Praise for *This Is Not the Life I Ordered*

"This book is an object lesson in the power of friendship—and the power of perseverance. The four fearless women who wrote it share their remarkable stories—featuring incredible highs and heartbreaking lows—and in the process show us how to overcome the fears that limit us. It's funny, inspiring, and practical—often all at the same time. Put the most entertaining episode of *TheView* in a blender with *Divine Secrets of the Ya-Ya Sisterhood*, and you'd get *This Is Not the Life I Ordered*. It's a book you'll want to order a stack of, so you can share it with your girlfriends and your daughters."

—Arianna Huffington, author of *On Becoming Fearless*

"I wish I had this book thirty years ago. What a welcome source of inspiration and insight."

—Linda Ellerbee, journalist, award-winning television producer, bestselling author, breast cancer survivor, and mom

"Even before you hear their stories, you feel their strength. When these four women came into my office, I knew I wanted to be a part of their mission. Readers will find themselves engulfed (in a good way) by their spirit."

—Gerry Laybourne, founder of Oxygen Media

"Kudos to the amazing strength of these women! This book is the needed inspiration to survive the worst luck and circumstances that catch women unexpectedly. Stories of almost unimaginable pain and tragedy: the death of loved ones, being witness to mass murder, the loss of an esteemed job after years of loyalty, and reversal of fortunes. But more importantly, these are stories of individual strength to transform shock, despair, and paralysis into . . . unexpected happiness."

—Amy Tan, bestselling author of *The Joy Luck Club*

"A must-read for all women and the men who love them."

—Rita Moreno, actor and winner of an Oscar, Emmy, Grammy, Tony, and the Presidential Medal of Freedom

"This book captures real-life moments—from overwhelming hardships to triumphant outcomes. It echoes hope on every page and gives insightful inspiration to get us through life's daily challenges. I love this book and all the threads of wisdom intricately sewn through each page. Best of all it is done with girlfriends—who have been my greatest support system. After you read it, you will realize that so much of your potential is just waiting to be released."

—Debbi Fields, founder of Mrs. Fields Cookies

"This is the book you need when it is 2:00 a.m., and you can't sleep because things in your life are not the way you hoped they would be. It is filled with the support and wisdom you would get from your friends, and more. It contains inspiring and true stories as well as the tools to help you move to the other side of whatever obstacles might confront you. It will comfort you and give you courage."

—Anne Robinson, cofounder of Windham Hill Records

"These women inspire us to go for the gold in our lives. They all deserve 10s!"

—Kristi Yamaguchi, gold medalist figure skater

"A moving book, full of hope and encouragement. I laughed and cried but always felt uplifted!"

—Jessica McClintock, founder and CEO of Jessica McClintock, Inc.

"You'll want to buy a copy of this book for yourself and every woman you care about. The inspiring real-life stories prove that you can overcome anything life throws at you, if you put your mind to it. These refreshingly honest stories will buoy your spirits and give you the clarity and courage to make your life what you want it to be now, not someday. Read it and reap."

—Sam Horn, bestselling author of *Tongue Fu!*

THIS IS NOT LIFE I ORDERED

Deborah Collins **STEPHENS**

Michealene Cristini **RISLEY**

Jan **YANEHIRO**

Jackie **SPEIER**

60 Ways to Keep Your Head Above Water When Life Keeps Dragging You Down

Foreword by Rita Moreno

Conari Press

This edition first published in 2019 by Conari Press, an imprint of

Red Wheel/Weiser, LLC
With offices at:
65 Parker Street, Suite 7
Newburyport, MA 01950
www.redwheelweiser.com

ISBN: 978-1-57324-737-5

Library of Congress Cataloging-in-Publication Data available upon request.

Cover design by Kathryn Sky-Peck
Interior illustrations © John Grimes
Interior by Deborah Dutton
Typeset in ITC Garamond, Gill Sans, and Trajan

Printed in Canada
MAR

10 9 8 7 6 5 4 3 2 1

This book is dedicated to brave and courageous women who light the dark for all of us.

Life is good. Life is short. May you achieve your dreams. May you also be wise enough and generous enough and kind enough to help another woman achieve hers.

THE AUTHORS

CONTENTS

CHAPTER THREE
MAKE COURAGE AN EVERYDAY COMPANION 69

CHAPTER FOUR
UNDERSTANDING MONEY 93

CHAPTER NINE
REBOUNDING FROM MISTAKES, MISERY, AND MAYHEM 171

CHAPTER TEN
DESIGNING YOUR LIFE 183

CHAPTER ELEVEN
LIGHT A CANDLE IN THE DARK 189

ACKNOWLEDGMENTS

It takes a village for a woman to pick herself up, dust herself off, and rise. We are indebted to the village of women who shared their stories with us. Their contributions have made for a good book. More important, they have enriched our lives in ways that will stay with us forever.

Our families give us meaning in so many ways that to go into detail would require that we write another book! To our children, Aaron and Lily Stephens; Christopher, Austin, and Dillon Risley; Jackson and Stephanie Sierra; Jaclyn, Jenna (Robinson), and J. B. Zimmerman; Meredith (Flynn) and Christopher Eves—thank you for being the loves of our lives!

To Greg Brandenburgh, our editor at Conari Press, thank you for your support and sense of humor. If the publishing doesn't work out, we're convinced that stand-up comedy can become your next act!

Finally, John Grimes *(www.grimescartoons.com)*, the funniest man we know, you read every word of our manuscript and delivered illustrations that make women laugh every time!

INTRODUCTION TO THE SECOND EDITION: HOPE REMAINS A STRATEGY (ALWAYS)

You may encounter many defeats, but you must not be defeated. It is necessary to encounter the defeats so you can know who you are, what you can rise from.

MAYA ANGELOU, AMERICAN POET (1928–2014)

What started around a kitchen table with nothing more than the goal of re-inventing ourselves has resulted in a community of women who still contact us with their stories. We thank you. We feel privileged to write a book that gives hope, inspiration, encouragement, and lessons for all women—anywhere, anytime, at any age. Hope remains a strategy—always.

This edition enters a world that feels like a runaway train and, on many days, a complete train wreck! In 2008, our paperback edition came roaring into a world where headlines screamed that we had entered the worst financial crisis since the Great Depression. Truly, it was a time that few of us saw coming and none of us ordered. Yet, survive we did.

We wrote this book because of the great upheaval and discord in the world. The polarization in our communities adds to the anxiety that far too many women face on a daily basis. We believe that each time a woman rises in the midst of difficult circumstances, our world heals. This book is our contribution to that healing.

WHAT'S NEW?

Promise me you will not spend so much time treading water and trying to keep your head above the waves that you truly forget how much you have always loved to swim.

TYLER KNOTT GREGSON, AMERICAN AUTHOR (1981–)

Since the first edition of our book, we have learned some new lessons that we've added to this second edition. We're excited to introduce you to women who have made comebacks and created remarkable lives. We're excited to share advances in science that have supported many of the lessons we recommended in our first book. And we've added our children's voices by sharing their experiences as they lived the lives we did not order. We hope their hard-earned wisdom will help others. In this edition, you'll also find new chapters on resilience, accompanied by steps and plans for designing a life that brings you joy. To help you in that endeavor, we've expanded the tools, tactics, and lessons on grief and loss.

We are living in the age of empowerment, where the Women's Marches, Time's Up, and MeToo movements show what can happen when women come together to make tomorrow better than today. There is no better time than now to form your own kitchen-table group, whether in person or online, to create a place where women can come together to support one another. This book gives a road map for creating your own group and a framework for sparking your motivation.

WHO ARE WE?

It's ok if you fall down and lose your spark. Just make sure that when you get back up, you rise as the whole damn fire.

ANONYMOUS

Life is a never-ending series of changes—both good and bad, and often indifferent. Together, we've learned to navigate and survive them. You may be thinking: Who are these women? What are their credentials? Well, we are not psychologists (although we have seen a few). We are not self-help experts (although we have read their books). We don't profess to have discovered any ultimate truths. We are simply four women who have banded together to help each other on our journey through life.

Jan Yanehiro says: "My divorce is final and I am gloriously single! The death of my first husband was terribly sad and awful, but I found divorce far worse. I keep saying that the next book I write will be *This Is Not the Husband I Ordered*. Change creates new opportunity—and a great one landed in my lap when I was asked to start a brand new School of Multimedia Communications for the Academy of Art University in San Francisco. When I accepted the directorship, I said to Elisa Stephens, the president of the university: 'You know, I'm old and I'm bossy . . . and I can make this happen for you!' Life is full. If I ever need a safety net, my girlfriends are there and I am grateful."

Jackie Speier lost her election for Lt. Governor of California by less than three points and ended her term as a state senator. Taking a job in a law firm with a dogged determination to continue in public service, but with no clear path for doing so, Jackie had a "desire versus destiny" moment. She ran for the 14th Congressional District seat in the US House of Representatives and won! "Always expect the unexpected or at least be prepared," Jackie says. Now serving in her tenth year in the House, Jackie has become a national figure on issues of sexual harassment, gun violence, and attacks upon our democracy by foreign interests.

Michealene Cristini Risley took a trip to Africa—and it wasn't a vacation. She went in search of a story on the terrible plight of young women and children in Zimbabwe. Arrested and interrogated by Zimbabwean officials, Michealene and her crew were imprisoned and then thrown out of the country. She continued her work as a human rights activist and her documentary, *Tapestries of Hope*, won multiple awards. She is the CEO at Curiosity Ink Media, where she is building media franchises and creating wholesome kids' entertainment. With her husband, Eric, and together with their children, Christopher, Austin, and Dillon, they have realized that home is truly where the heart is.

Deborah Collins Stephens's husband died; then her daughter graduated from college. "I'm learning to live alone after being married for thirty-three years," she says. When her son, Aaron, married, Deborah walked him down the aisle, gaining a daughter-in-law whom she adores. The sorting through of possessions—moving from a large house into a small bungalow—carried over into her work. "Now, I only choose to spend my time with people and on projects that I truly love," she says. "I've earned that right!" Deborah continues to consult in leadership development and is an executive coach—but only with women leaders. Why? "Simply because we need more of them and I'm committed to doing my part," she affirms.

Thank you for reading our book. May you climb into a new life and achieve your dreams. Know that we will be cheering you on.

Deborah Collins Stephens
Michealene Cristini Risley
Jackie Speier
Jan Yanehiro

PREFACE:
SLIGHTLY LESS THAN
WORST-CASE SCENARIOS

Whether one is twenty, forty, or sixty; whether one has suc-
ceeded, failed, or just muddled along; whether yesterday
was full of sun or storm, or one of those dull days with no
weather at all, life begins again each morning in the heart
of a woman.

LEIGH MITCHELL HODGES, POET (1876–1954)

We are simply four women whom destiny threw together.
Collectively, we have experienced the extreme joys and deep
sorrows that life offers up—from mundane moments to the
dramatic and surreal. We have a history of six marriages,
one divorce, ten children, four stepchildren, six dogs, two
miscarriages, two cats, twelve koi fish, a failed adoption,
widowhood, two parakeets, and foster-parenthood. We have
built companies, lost companies, and sold companies. One
of us was shot and left for dead on the tarmac in South
America, and three of us have lived through the deaths
of spouses.

We've raised babies and teenagers and are still alive to
talk about it. We've had our hearts broken by affairs and
mended through our friendships. We've known celebrity

and loneliness, along with self-doubt and near financial ruin. We've been caregivers to those who faced terminal illnesses and supporters of those who lost loved ones.

We grew up in less-than-wealthy families, where living paycheck to paycheck was the norm. We've known more wealth than our parents could ever have imagined, and we've lost more money than they ever made! Forced to be creative, we have raised families on bare budgets and at times have been the sole breadwinners when our spouses were unemployed, seriously ill, or dying. In our careers, we've often been the only women at the table. We have taken risks that bet the company, bet the election, and—in some cases—bet the house!

(A COLLECTION OF MISFORTUNATE EVENTS)

        THIS IS NOT THE LIFE I ORDERED

When Bad Things Happen to Smart Women

A reporter once jokingly referred to our collection of misfortunate events as the female version of the book of Job, almost expecting that a hoard of locusts would descend on us at any moment! Yet, we do not view our lives with sadness or remorse. We see them as gifts, filled with events that have helped us develop a razor-sharp sense of what counts and what simply doesn't. Time and again, we have learned to reinvent ourselves. The process of reinvention, we now know, is best managed with humor, friendship, optimism, and a long-lasting high-beam flashlight to see the light at the end of every tunnel.

Among us, there is one commonality: loss. We've experienced the heartbreaking loss of lives, along with the loss of a marriage, a child, of innocence, and of money, stability, and hope. Loss causes formidable transitions that touch every woman at some point. But loss should never be faced alone and so we created a monthly meeting around our kitchen tables to share our lives and to support and encourage one another. These kitchen-table conversations were always therapeutic and inspiring. Our conversations gave us hope and inner strength. We knew that together, as friends, we would never walk alone.

Kitchen-Table Friends

Word spread about our kitchen-table conversations. We were asked to speak at conferences and to women's groups. We titled our talk "Survive and Thrive: Ten Turbo-Charged Tips for Women in Transition" and guessed that maybe thirty people might show up for the conversation.

Over 400 women came to our first session, forcing the fire marshals to lock the doors! We told our stories that day. Women lined up to talk with us. They shared their own personal versions of "survive-and-thrive" lives. Weeks later, we were encouraged to write a book. More conference organizers asked us to speak. We used the idea of writing a book as an excuse to continue our monthly meetings, yet wrote not a single word.

In fact, we continued to meet for over a decade before we put one word onto paper for that imaginary book we told everyone we were writing! We talked about losing businesses, losing husbands, and wanting to lose husbands. We talked about building careers, building families, and building on our fragile networking skills. We talked about finding our self-esteem, finding our paths, even finding new mates. We talked about challenges, taking risks, and taking a chance on love again. We talked candidly about near financial ruin, actual financial ruin, and avoiding financial ruin. We talked about our children, our co-workers, our colleagues, and our sex lives. We left no topic unexplored.

We encouraged one another through the numerous transitions we were experiencing. We even gave ourselves a name—Women in Transition, WIT for short—noting that we would truly need our collective wit to navigate through these tricky times. In time, our meetings took the form of what we envisioned as a quilting circle in the Wild West. Yet the fabric we wove at our meetings was the fabric of our lives.

We learned many lessons in our decades-long friendship. We learned that we had been fooled. We had convinced ourselves that, if we could manage our schedules, break through the glass ceiling, spend quality time with our families, bring home the bacon (and fry it up in a pan) while bouncing children on our hips and creating warm and loving relationships with our husbands, in-laws, and colleagues, somehow, some way, we would be rewarded with the problem-free lives that had eluded us. We were wrong.

Surviving and Thriving

From kitchen conversations to the thousands of conversations we've had with women all over the world, we learned that the problem-free life we sought was worse than just an illusion. It was a life-depleting myth to which too many have fallen victim. A woman's life is about much more than success, having it all, or the elusive balance we all seek (and may find). It is about more than seeking perfection or conquering the world (although you may). It is about more than gritting your teeth and making it through (no matter how). It is about surviving and thriving.

For us, surviving and thriving meant reinventing and rebuilding, and realizing that success is never final and failure is never fatal. It meant putting our best foot forward and walking into a future we had designed. All too often, the tiny voice inside us revealed that, although we might look like pillars of success on the outside, our teenagers were out of control, our jobs could end tomorrow, and our spouses, colleagues, and bosses were often untruthful, selfish, unfaithful, had died, or were just plain stupid.

Surviving and thriving meant taking what life offered up while searching for the opportunities, the joy, and the compassion in less-than-pleasant and always less-than-perfect circumstances. Together, we would navigate through some tricky times.

So, How's Your Life?

Our collective lives have been filled with more transitions than we thought possible. Transitions are an important part of the fabric of every woman's life. They affect us individually, but also have a ripple effect on our families. Transitions can build our characters and turn us into wise women, or they can leave us feeling depressed and alone. Successful transitions can make us strong—ready to extend a helpful hand to other women—or they can make us fearful of what lies ahead.

We offer this book as a road map of sorts for life's transitions. It contains the many lessons we've learned on how to ride the tidal waves of change that often engulf women. We've boiled those lessons down into sixty imperatives for surviving the vicissitudes of life and thriving despite them. Along the way, we have been honored to meet many magnificent and brave women whose stories of challenge, resilience, and triumph we include as examples of hope for all of us. This book is a literary kitchen table, where we invite you to pull up a chair and join us so you don't have to go through life alone. We hope this inspiring circle of women gives you hope, insight, and inspiration to deal with your own challenges and changes.

Education is not enough if it's not accompanied by action. With that in mind, each section in our book ends with suggested action plans and tools to help you implement them. We call this section the WIT Kit, and we hope you find these insights valuable. More important, we hope you'll be motivated to adapt them and apply them in your own lives, where they can produce real-world results.

We know you're busy. We know you're probably running from the minute you wake until bedtime. But we also know that taking time to follow up on the recommendations found in the WIT Kit can make the difference between merely surviving what life throws at you and thriving *despite* what life throws at you.

Some of the actions described in the WIT Kit take only a few minutes. Some involve more time and planning. All of them can help. If you feel as if life is dragging you down, these actions can help you keep your head above water. They can help you create a higher quality of life for yourself and your loved ones—now, not someday.

Deborah Collins Stephens
Michealene Cristini Risley
Jackie Speier
Jan Yanehiro
San Francisco, California, July 2018

FOREWORD

There are fifteen people in the world who have won an Emmy, a Grammy, an Oscar, and a Tony. Rita Moreno is one of them. Former President Barack Obama referred to Rita, the only Latina to win the awards, as a trailblazer with the courage to break through barriers and forge new paths. Supreme Court Justice Sonia Sotomayor said: "When I was younger, I idolized Rita Moreno. I still do."

Rita is a role model for millennials and an icon of inspiration for all generations. Today, at eighty-six, with retirement not in her DNA, Rita has a hit television show—*One Day at a Time*—and even more awards: a Kennedy Center honor, honors from the ACLU and Ellis Island for her work in civil rights, along with cover stories in *Time, Newsweek, Glamour,* and the *Today* show. Her path to fame and success has not been an easy one, however. Rita has lived most every lesson in this book and come out the other side stronger, wiser, and more accomplished. Here, in her own words, is how she describes the journey.

Just Deal with It

When I first read *This Is Not the Life I Ordered*, I told the publisher that it was a must-read for all women and the men who love them. In the stories and lessons, I saw many parallels with my own life. When Jan asked me to write the Foreword, I immediately said yes. These four women epitomize how I and many women cope: We just deal with it. In my book, *Rita Moreno—A Memoir*, I begin with that advice: Just deal with it. I spent a good part of my life looking for an identity that was safe. I didn't want to be this "Latina girl." I didn't want to be this "sexpot."

I had no role models, so I chose one: Elizabeth Taylor. In retrospect, we all know that is simply not possible; it's not feasible. It doesn't work. What happens as a result is that you live a very muddled life with respect to identity. You lose something extremely valuable and important—self-respect. This struggle was very painful. I always tell women today to be themselves and let the chips fall where they may.

You Don't Die from Not Being Liked

I was always the darling, please-like-me kid. It's the immigrant syndrome; it comes from being Puerto Rican, from being on the outside. For me and for so many women, we are told in subtle and not so subtle ways: "Don't make waves; don't make noise." My mother was very conscious of that. I was brought up trying to please the world. I wanted the world to like me. The greatest lesson I ever learned is that you don't die from not being liked. Yet there is always the little voice or dark presence that stays with you forever. She's the one who, still to this day, says things like: "Ha-ha, I told you that you couldn't do it." In me, she still exists and I have a feeling that creature exists in a lot of women. They just don't think of her as an entity, but I do. I call this voice my Rosarita. I just send her to her room all the time. It's impossible to get rid of her, but I've learned not to let her run my life.

Perseverancia

I had won the Oscar and a Golden Globe for *West Side Story*. I fully believed that, after that, I was going to get a lot of work and that everything was going to be just rosy. The opposite happened. I couldn't get a job to save my life. I couldn't believe it. It just absolutely broke my heart. Today at eighty-six, I look back on those events as recompense for all the hard years in a profession that challenged my sense of dignity and self-worth at every turn. I am reminded that, in this third act of my life, the falling down and getting up is very much a part of the American Dream.

This Is Not the Life I Ordered is filled to the brim with stories of falling down and getting back up. What I say to my *gente* [people] is to hang on, and to remember who you are. Be proud of who you are, and keep talking. And keep complaining. And just don't ever—ever—give up. I call this not giving up *perseverancia* and it means perseverance. There is nothing more powerful than a woman who embodies perseverance. The lessons in this book and the women who wrote them exhibit perseverancia in all that they do. The wonderful thing about perseverancia is that it is open to all of us, no matter our background or socio-economic status.

My good friend, the brilliant author Amy Tan, said that *This Is Not the Life I Ordered* gives women the inspiration to survive the worst luck and circumstances and to climb into a new life with unexpected happiness. That is what I wish for every woman—the ability to survive and thrive.

Rita Moreno

CHAPTER ONE

MANAGING MISFORTUNE

*If one woman sees another woman
as successful, that woman will
never fail, never feel alone.*

**FLORENCE SCOVEL SHINN,
WRITER (1871–1940)**

1
CONVENE A GATHERING OF KITCHEN-TABLE FRIENDS.

You are the storyteller of your own life and you can create the legend or not.

ISABEL ALLENDE, CHILEAN-AMERICAN WRITER (1942–)

Find One Safe Place to Tell Your Story

The first and most important way to keep your head above water when life threatens to drag you down is to create a safe place where your stories can be heard—a gathering of kitchen-table friends. Gathering around a kitchen table and telling our own stories was empowering. While we didn't know it at the time, we were "bearing witness" to one another by talking about our experiences in a trusted environment. Psychologists tell us that "bearing witness" is a vital ingredient in the healing process.

We looked forward to our gatherings because we knew that they provided the one place in our lives where we would be heard—a place and time where women would listen without judgment. We have no doubt that being able to tell our stories saved our sanity and, in some cases, saved our lives. We believe that every woman needs to create for herself a safe place where her story can be heard. We know from our own experience that staying connected with each other has made all the difference in our ability to cope with the challenges we've faced.

Think you don't have time for your women friends? We encourage you to think again. If you're thinking that you don't feel up to doing this right now, that's precisely why you ought to do this. If your energy is low, it's because you're trying to do everything by yourself. You're running on empty, and you need to fill up your emotional tank with support and input from women who care about you. Your own kitchen-table group will feed your soul. You can get started today by following these seven simple steps to create a wonderful network of women friends.

Seven Steps for Forming a Kitchen-Table Group

1. ***Reach out:*** No matter how bad your life may be right now, plan a get-together with women you admire. They do not need to be famous, rich, or fabulously accomplished. You do not need to know them well, although they do need to be women you respect and who share similar values and priorities—women with integrity who will be willing to listen, give encouragement, and be honest. Many women feel just as isolated as you do. Now is the perfect time to get to know that mom who shares car-pool duties with you. What about the woman at work with whom you have only a nodding acquaintance but have always felt a spark of connection? Perhaps there's someone on a fundraising committee you've admired, someone who can always be counted on to do what she says she's going to do.

2. ***Choose a location:*** Pick a meeting place that has comfortable surroundings and that gives you privacy. It can be the corner of a local coffee shop, or the living room of your home. The kitchen tables in our different homes have worked well for us all these years.

3. ***Set a first meeting:*** You don't have to do anything fancy. Just pick up the phone, send an email, or ask in person. Tell the women up front that you know they're busy, that the purpose of this meeting is to create a support network that meets regularly where women can talk out what's going on in their lives in a confidential setting. Participants are welcome to talk about their jobs (or lack of a job), their families, their health, and their finances—whatever is on their minds and in their hearts. Give your group a name and commit to meeting regularly (every other week, or at least monthly). In our own group, we

meet monthly but sometimes convene more often when one of our members is in the midst of a crisis.

4. **_Set ground rules:_** The first few meetings of your kitchen-table group can probably benefit from some sort of structure. In our group meetings, we always begin with some illuminating questions:

   - So, how's your life?

   - How can we help?

   - Who do we know who can help?

   - What are you happy about right now in your life?

   - What is there to laugh about?

   - When we leave here today, what three things are we committing to each other that we will do for ourselves?

5. **_Stay positive:_** Do not allow your group to turn into a "pity party." Pity parties rob you of your spirit and do nothing to empower you. The purpose of this gathering is not simply to complain, and stop there. Go ahead and get what's bothering you, worrying you, or hurting you off your chest, and then ask for advice. Brainstorm possible solutions and strategies for the issues you're facing.

6. **_Use the WIT Kit:_** The suggestions found at the end of each section in this book can provide a focus for your meetings. We purposely created the WIT Kit to give you tools that you can work with as a group in your own kitchen-table meetings. Discuss the topics and questions among yourselves.

7. **_Share your experiences:_** Visit our website, _www.kitchen tablefriends.com,_ and let us know your stories.

Our kitchen-table group met for over ten years and, during that time, we told many stories, solved many problems, and mended many broken hearts. We begin by introducing you to the defining moments that brought us together as lifelong friends.

2
TRANSCEND MISFORTUNATE EVENTS.

Although there may be tragedy in your life, there's always a possibility to triumph. It doesn't matter who you are, where you come from. The ability to triumph begins with you. Always.

OPRAH WINFREY, TV HOST (1954–)

Jungle Encounter

"Nightmares. They still invade my sleep forty years later. The nightmares remind me that life is a precious resource to be used up, enjoyed, lived. I am Jackie Speier, and my nightmares take me back to a fateful November day in 1978. I was twenty-eight and getting ready to purchase my first home. I was legislative counsel to a US congressman and I had it all! I also had a strong premonition that the trip I was arranging to South America could be one from which I might not return. 'Silly thoughts,' my friend Katy assured me. 'After all, you will be traveling with the press corps and a US congressman. What could possibly happen?'

"Holed up in a congressional office for hours at a time, I was reading State Department briefings on a religious community created by the Reverend Jim Jones. We were investigating numerous allegations from relatives that their family members were being held against their will in a jungle hideaway known as the People's Temple. As we reviewed taped interviews with defectors, I had an ominous feeling—a feeling I could not put out of my mind. One former member had told us that people were being forced to act out suicides in an exercise Jones called the White Night.

"Congressman Leo Ryan, my boss, had heard enough. He decided to see firsthand the plight of US citizens in Guyana. But even after the CIA and the State Department had cleared the trip for safety, I still had doubts.

"We flew into Guyana's capital, Georgetown, changed planes, and continued on to Port Kaituma—a remote airstrip deep in the South American jungle. A convoy of several trucks drove us to the Jonestown encampment. We entered a clearing in the jungle, where I saw an outdoor amphitheater surrounded by small cabins. You couldn't help but be impressed by the settlement. In less than two years, a community had been carved out of dense jungle. During our first and only night at the People's Temple, the members entertained us with music and singing. I remember looking into the eyes of Jim Jones—and I saw madness there. He was no longer the charismatic leader who had lured more than 900 people to a remote jungle commune; he was a man possessed.

"The congressman and I randomly selected people to interview to determine whether they were being held against their will. Many of the individuals were young—eighteen or nineteen years old—while others were senior citizens. One by one, each confirmed that they loved living in the People's Temple. It was almost as if they had been coached to answer our questions. As the night drew to a close, NBC news correspondent Don Harris walked off alone to smoke a cigarette. In the darkness, two people approached him and put notes into his hand. Harris gave the notes to me, and I held in my hands evidence of what I had sensed all along: These people were indeed being held against their will in this South American compound.

"Morning broke, and I interviewed the two people who had given Harris the notes saying they wanted to leave. Word of the opportunity to leave had gotten out, and more people started coming forward saying that they also wanted to leave. Then suddenly, a couple of men with guns appeared.

THIS IS NOT THE LIFE I ORDERED

Chaos ensued as more people approached us wanting to leave. Jim Jones started ranting and screaming. Larry Layton, one of Jones' closest assistants, said: 'Don't get the wrong idea. We are all very happy here. You see the beauty of this special place.' One hour later, Larry Layton had become one of the defectors, asking to escape the jungle compound."

3
WHEN LEFT ON THE TARMAC, START WALKING.

The world is round and the place which may seem like the end may also be only the beginning.

IVY BAKER PRIEST, FORMER US SECRETARY OF THE TREASURY (1905–1975)

Three Minutes from Death

"People began screaming and crying, some parents engaging in a tug-of-war over their children—one wanting to go; the other wanting to stay. So many people had decided to escape the People's Temple that the consulate had to order another plane.

"We left for the airstrip. Dressed in an oversized yellow poncho, Larry Layton, Jones' assistant, seemed overly eager to board the cargo plane. I distrusted him and asked that he be searched before boarding. A journalist patted him down, but did not find the gun Layton had hidden under his poncho. Thinking back, I now realize how helpless we were—a congressman, congressional aides, journalists, and cameramen; not one among us a police officer or military escort. We had nothing to protect us other than the imagined shield of the invulnerability of a US congressman and members of the US press corps.

"Suddenly, we heard a scream. Seconds later, I heard an unfamiliar noise. I saw people running into the bushes and realized that the noise was gunfire. I dropped to the ground and curled up around a wheel of the plane, pretending to be dead. I heard footsteps. I felt my body twitch as someone pumped bullets into me at point-blank range. I was shot five times.

"The gunmen continued to walk around the tarmac, shooting innocent people. Soon it was quiet. I opened my eyes and looked down at my body. A bone was sticking out of my arm, and blood was everywhere. I remember thinking: My God, I am twenty-eight years old and I am about to die. I yelled out for Congressman Ryan, calling his name several times. There was no answer.

"The plane's engine was still revving, and I thought that if I could just get to the cargo hatch, I could escape this place. I crawled toward the opening, dragging my body as close as I could to the baggage compartment. A reporter from the *Washington Post* picked me up and put me into the cargo hold. I remember asking him if he could give me something to stop my bleeding, and he gave me his shirt. I was losing so much blood that the shirt was soaked in seconds.

"The plane was filled with bullet holes, and we soon realized that it would never make it out of this hell on earth. Someone pulled me out of the plane and placed me back on the airstrip. Accidentally, they laid my head upon an anthill and ants started crawling all over me. Lying next to me was a reporter's tape recorder. I taped a last message to my parents and brother, telling them that I loved them.

"Supposedly, the Guyanese Army was going to secure the airstrip and rescue us, so I held on tightly to the belief that the army would come. It grew dark, and we continued to wait. Although I was in excruciating pain, I clung to life.

"In the middle of the night, word reached those on the tarmac that there had been a mass suicide at the People's Temple. At one o'clock the next day, twenty hours after the shootings, the Guyanese Air Force arrived. Their arrival coincided with a message to the world that more than 900 people, including a US congressman and members of his delegation, were dead. The headlines called it the worst mass suicide in history. To this day, I still refer to the events at Jonestown as a mass murder.

"The Guyanese Air Force transported the survivors to a waiting US Air Force Medivac plane. Etched in my mind is the memory of how I felt at that very moment, as if someone had wrapped me in the American flag. I was so grateful.

"Loaded with survivors, the Air Force plane set off for the United States. As we taxied down the runway, I recall glancing down at my body. It seemed so surreal, as if the mangled lump of flesh belonged to someone other than me. Months later, I was told that the medical technician who tended to me during the flight said that I was three minutes from death."

One Step Forward, One Day at a Time

"When we finally arrived at Andrews Air Force Base, where I was immediately taken into surgery, I had developed gangrene, and surgeons debated whether to amputate my leg. After four hours of surgery, the nurse wheeled me out of the surgical ward, and there stood my mother, who had traveled from San Francisco to be with me. They told her that they needed to transfer me to the Baltimore Shock/Trauma Center to attempt to stem the spread of gangrene. I begged my mother and the doctors to transfer me by ambulance, fearing I would die on another plane flight.

"The shock/trauma center was lit with incredibly bright lights. Numerous IVs were hooked up to me. I remember asking the nurse how many calories there were in all the stuff that was flowing into my body."

"Three thousand," she replied.

"I said: 'Oh, my God, I am going to get so fat!' Interesting, isn't it, how we can lose perspective in the middle of trauma?

"After yet another surgery, I was returned to my hospital room. The surgeons had repaired my body, but my hair was still matted with dried blood, Guyanese dirt, and dead ants. In an act of love I will never forget, my brother tenderly washed my hair.

"The doctors remained very concerned about the gangrene in my wounds. In a last-ditch effort, they began a series of hyperbaric treatments that required me to be placed into a chamber that resembled an iron lung filled with anti-bacterial microbes and oxygen. Each time they removed me from the chamber, I vomited violently. Unfortunately, they had to repeat this process several times.

"Confident that they had beaten the gangrene, they transferred me back to Arlington Hospital, where I was placed under twenty-four-hour protection, with US Marshals posted outside my door. Threats had been made against my life by individuals associated with the People's Temple. They blamed the congressional investigation for the mass deaths in Guyana and wanted to retaliate.

"The surgeons performed skin grafts on my legs. The gunshots had blown apart my right arm, and a steel dowel was inserted to hold together what remained. The radial nerve in my arm was damaged, and I could not use my fingers or lift my arm. The first time they tried to get me on my feet to walk, I fainted. After being hospitalized for nearly two months and enduring ten surgeries, I was finally discharged and flew back to San Francisco.

"The days ahead were a flurry of interviews about the Jonestown massacre. I was not allowed to stay in my home because of the death threats, so I lived with a friend. I still carried two bullets in my body that doctors had deemed too risky to remove. I never appeared in public without layers of clothes to cover what I had begun to believe was my hideous, disfigured body. In the following years, I would endure months of physical therapy to regain the use of my arm.

"I was twenty-eight, a single woman who could hardly feed herself and whose body was maimed and scarred. One day, I realized that if I was going to get over this—if I was ever going to move forward—I had to figure out a way not to wallow in self-pity.

"The exact moment I came to terms with what had happened in Guyana occurred years later, on a crowded beach in Hawaii. The disfigured body I walked in was mine. The joy I felt at just being alive had become greater than my insecurities. I had come to realize that a person's body was irrelevant and physical beauty was a shallow concern. I was disabled, but I did not believe that a disability of any kind prevented me from living a full and wonderful life. If anything, my disfigurement had opened my eyes to the bias often harbored toward those who are different.

"I put on a bathing suit that day and walked across the Hawaiian beach as people stared at the scars of my gunshot wounds. I just kept walking. And I learned with every step that, as difficult as it may be, you just have to take the next step. You just have to force yourself to do it. In the jungle on that November day, it was not my turn to die. But certainly now was my time to live."

Life Gives No Guarantees

"I survived the massacre in Guyana and went on to marry an emergency-room physician. I was also elected to serve in the California legislature. We had our first child and life was turning out to be just as I had dreamed. We tried for more children, but after two miscarriages, a failed adoption, and fertility treatments, Steve and I decided to give up on our dream of another child. I launched a statewide campaign to become California's Secretary of State. Miraculously, three months later, I found myself pregnant in what doctors termed a high-risk pregnancy. I promptly withdrew from the campaign to focus on the health of our unborn child.

"On a rainy January day, three months into my pregnancy, I was en route to Sacramento when my secretary tracked me down to tell me that Steve had been in a car accident. I immediately phoned the emergency room and talked with the attending physician. I could tell by his voice that my husband's injuries were severe and I was an hour away. As I rushed back to the hospital, I feared the worst.

"Once I arrived, it seemed like hours before they would let me see Steve. When I finally got to see him in the ICU, he had a shunt in his head and was on a respirator. His body was warm, but the machines indicated he had no brain function. I kissed him. I held him. I told him I loved him, even though I knew he couldn't hear me. I couldn't believe that yet another nightmare was unfolding in front of me.

"I later learned that an uninsured driver with faulty brakes had careened through a stop sign, broadsiding Steve's car. His carelessness killed a talented, caring, vital man. I was now a pregnant widow with a young son.

"The loss of my husband was traumatic. I no longer even wanted to get out of bed. Yet, I really had no choice. I was the sole supporter of two children, one yet unborn. Steve had no life insurance, so his death was both an emotional and a financial disaster. I had to sell everything, including my home. I spent the next eight years as a single mother raising two children.

"Today, many years later, I am fortunate to live with great joy and happiness. I am married to a wonderful man, Barry Dennis, whom I met on a blind date. He was a confirmed bachelor, yet, five months later, we were engaged! My children are now happy, well-adjusted, and healthy adults.

"I want women to remember that, when life leaves them alone on the tarmac—whether it be the devastating loss of a loved one, the shattering of a lifelong dream, the loss of a job, or events that turn the world upside down— they can always learn to walk again. I am living proof that women can reinvent and rebuild their lives, no matter what hardships they have faced."

4

WHEN LIFE IS NOT WHAT YOU ORDERED, BEGIN AGAIN.

One of the hardest things you will ever have to do, my dear, is to grieve the loss of a person who is still alive.

ANONYMOUS

Death and Divorce

"It's been twenty-three years since my husband, John Zimmerman, died of Stage 4 glioblastoma, the most aggressive type of brain cancer," says Jan Yanehiro.

"He was forty-six; I was forty-seven. We had been married for twenty-two years. Our children were twelve, ten, and six years old when we lost him. I'm pleased to say that the children grew up to be fabulous adults and I am still working (and loving it) at seventy.

"And for the record, yes, I think about John—often. I miss him especially when I realize how many special moments he missed in our children's lives—driver's licenses, prom dates, acting in school plays, attending swim meets and Lacrosse games, summer jobs, high school graduations, college graduations, post-college jobs, and our daughter's wedding. Tears spring to my eyes in unexpected moments— moments like right now as I write this.

"Two and a half years after John died, I remarried. The marriage lasted ten years and ended in divorce. Someone once asked me which was harder, to lose a husband to death or divorce? Without hesitation, I answered: Divorce! Okay, maybe without the exclamation point, but divorce was harder.

"Death is final. There's nothing you can do about it. John didn't want to die. He felt sure he was going to beat brain cancer. He didn't. Divorce is hurtful, scathing, and full of betrayal. That betrayal cuts so deep that, even ten years later, I am only beginning to feel that the wounds are less deep. I think that means that I'm healing. One curious person asked me why I had gotten a divorce. My answer was simple: He cheated on me.

"If I sound so firm, so sure, so clear as I write about this now, I wasn't then. It took me years (and years) to process the divorce. I am still embarrassed to say I *am* divorced! I find it hard even to admit *who filed* for divorce. He did. I feel like such a wimp that I didn't do it first.

"It's been eleven years since I moved out of our home—a move I made against everyone's best advice, including my divorce attorney. My ex-husband filed for divorce and moved into the guesthouse. Each day, each night, each week, I was a mess and my self-esteem hit rock bottom. Jackie told me I was acting like an emotionally abused wife. Of course, I denied it. Me? No, not me. I had a career in television; I had three children and three stepchildren. I was on a corporate board. Abused?

"The short answer is yes, I was. To be clear, there was no physical abuse. But emotional abuse? Yes. When I got an email from my ex, I felt nauseous and was scared even to open it. I could feel my heart pounding when I did. What does he want now? What is his new demand? Arbitration? Settlement? How did I fail this marriage? When your self-esteem slips to below zero, it's amazing what a simple email can do to you.

"It's been nine years since my divorce became final. It took me two years to get the divorce, and it cost me $250,000. (I didn't have that kind of money, so I borrowed it.) And I wasn't even asking for alimony. We had signed a post-nuptial agreement about a year before the divorce because he claimed he wanted to protect his company. Foolishly, I signed. During the divorce, his attorney brought up that business was bad for the company and my ex was actually contemplating asking me for alimony!

"A year ago, I paid off all the borrowed money for my divorce to attorneys, mediators, accountants, and real estate appraisers. In the end, I just wanted to be done! Done with all the hurt, uncertainty, and anger. A good family friend,

Larry Howell, gave me great advice: 'If you want it to be done, you make it be done.'

"Did I leave money on the table? Probably. Do I feel everything was fair? No. What did I get? I got half of the value of the home I had invested in. But I reached the point where I could say to myself: I feel pretty darn good! Finally. On most days, I feel like the happiest single woman in all of San Francisco! I turned seventy years wiser. I can't say seventy years old, because I don't *feel* old. I mean, not old like we thought we would be . . . wrinkled, gray, bent over, wobbly, babbling souls. Sure, I have wrinkles and I am gray. However, my hairdresser makes sure I return to my 'natural born' color every five weeks!

"I feel I am just hitting my stride! Gosh, it feels good to say it and to *feel* it as well. My three children are all grown up. And I'm mighty proud to be their mother. On the morning John died, I made two promises. I promised John that I would make sure our children grew up happy, got an education, and *lived* their lives. And I promised myself that my children would *not* use the death of their father as an excuse for anything in their lives.

"My first-born, Jaclyn Mariko Zimmerman, is thirty-six, living and thriving in Berlin, Germany. Jaclyn is one of the bravest women I know. She lives fearlessly in a foreign land and creates her own job opportunities. Full speed ahead for my first-born!

Jenna Reiko Zimmerman is thirty-four years old. After ten years in New York City producing shows for the Food Network—she worked on seven Emmy-nominated shows and was herself nominated for an Emmy as one of the producers of *Guy's Big Bites*—she moved back to San Francisco. On her second day there, she met a young man named John Robinson whom I adore and who fits in perfectly as another member of our 'J-crew.' (My late husband John and I gave all our children names that start with the letter J.)

"My son, JB (John Blake) Zimmerman, is thirty and living the life of a bachelor in Santa Monica, California. He graduated from the University of Arizona and always knew he wanted a career in television and movie production. Like his dad (who was a CPA), he loves movies. The two of them watched movies together in the den from the time JB was about two. JB is working for several production companies that are defining what Millennials and Centennials want to see—short-form, online, and 24/7.

"The silver lining to my divorce is my two stepchildren, Meredith and Christopher Eves. I may be divorced from their father, but I choose not to be divorced from them. Meredith is married to a most wonderful person, Conor Flynn. They have two adorable children, Kieran and Gigi, and live in Connecticut. Chris is working in Los Angeles, making his mark on music videos."

Moving On

"A lot of people assumed that, since I worked in radio and television for more than twenty-five years, I would be set financially. Oh, how I wish that were true. Yes, I made a good living, but life interfered. I need to work to make sure that I can take care of myself in retirement. I loathe thinking that I might have to rely upon my children.

"I am a firm believer that you must tell the universe what you need. In 2008, I needed a job. The job goddess heard my plea, as a great job landed in my lap. The President of the Academy of Art University in San Francisco, Dr. Elisa Stephens, called me with an opportunity to start a brand new department—a School of Communications and Media Technologies.

"In two months (and with a lot of help), we built a studio, hired faculty, and designed a four-year degree program as well as a master's program. It's truly amazing how students can make you feel young and inspire you to re-invent yourself. As the founding director of the department, I'm having a blast! Of course, I've had to learn a new language that includes words like 'curriculum,' 'syllabus,' and 'rubrics.' I've made mistakes—bad hires, accepting student excuses too easily, cramming way too much information into one semester. But here's the good news: You *can* transfer your skills from one career to another. I'm a trained reporter; I'm always asking questions. And now, I'm asking questions of my students. What happened to that assignment? Why not take a risk? What is it that you really want to accomplish?"

Am I Dating … or Not?

"Not.

"At this point, if I have a free night, I'd rather spend it at home watching an episode of *This Is Us* rather than sitting across from a man in a restaurant and having to stroke yet another male ego! As my friend Mary Les Casto (Founder of Casto Travel—a global company) says: 'There's no man good enough for me. I'm good enough for me.' Here! Here!

"Did I mention that I redesigned my ring after my divorce? I decided that I deserved every karat of that diamond ring from my second husband, and I really wanted to wear it every day. But I didn't want the ring to be the same as when he gave it to me—too many unpleasant memories and bad karma too! I redesigned it and wear it on my right finger rather proudly every day.

"I may be alone, but I'm not lonely. Life is full. And I purposefully keep it that way. I continue to serve on the boards of Kristi Yamaguchi's Always Dream Foundation and the San Francisco-Osaka Sister City Association. I just went to Osaka to celebrate the sixtieth anniversary of the two cities' partnership. I also completed six years of service as chair of the Representation Project, whose mission is gender equality, and six years of service on the US-Japan Council. And after ten and a half years, I stepped down from the corporate board of the Bank of Marin.

"Last year, Deborah asked me to come to Indianapolis for her Indiana Conference for Women to interview Oscar-winning actress and author Diane Keaton. Interview *Annie Hall?* Yes, count me in! In reading Keaton's books, I learned that she is self-conscious about her thinning hair, that she refuses to get a face lift, and that she adopted her children when she was fifty and fifty-five. She told us on stage she is soon to be seventy-two. Bravo, Diane!

"At a recent dinner party, I was seated next to LeRoy Morishita, President of the California State University, East Bay, who told me there are no Asian-Americans on the Board of Trustees for the California State University system. I was appalled. I graduated from California State University, Fresno, so I have a particular interest. Hmmmm, I thought, I should toss my name into the pot as a potential Trustee. Women, we can't be shy; we must find a way to have a seat at the table. Stay tuned! I feel as if I'm just getting started!"

5
LEARN THE SECRETS OF THE BLUE-HAIRED LADY.

I was so far from the seat of power, but my naïveté worked to my advantage. When I was told that the studio passed on my first pilot, I thought that was a good thing—you know, like "passed" in college.

LINDA BLOODWORTH-THOMASON, TV PRODUCER AND WRITER (1947–)

Blue Hair on Fridays

"I wondered if he noticed her blue hair? He showed no reaction to the fact that the elderly woman sitting across from him in his opulent banker's office had just about the bluest hair he had ever seen. I am Deborah Stephens and that blue-haired lady was my grandmother .

"Her blue hair, combined with a matter-of-fact demeanor, penetrating eyes, and down-home hospitality, left no doubt that he, Mr. Banker, was just a minor obstacle standing between her and what she wanted—a loan. It never occurred to her that there were reasons she might not succeed: her lack of collateral (her home wasn't in her name), no credit rating, and the fact that, in those days (a mere thirty-some years ago), a woman could not even have a credit card in her own name. Nonetheless, I knew Mr. Banker was no match for the blue-haired lady.

"Her silver mop of hair was always tinted blue on Fridays—a tint, a curl, and a comb-out every Friday morning, no matter what. The whole process left her feeling beautiful, powerful, and bold. And so I came to love the blue hair almost as much as I loved her. I also grew up believing that all confident women of a certain age tinted their hair blue!

"That day was a defining moment for me. Yes, my grandmother received the loan—a college student loan, for me. Her negotiation skills could blow the doors open in any corporate boardroom. Yet she was uneducated and poor. Her wealth was comprised of deep religious beliefs and unconditional kindness. She also possessed the tenacity of a bulldog, as she never let the word 'no' stand in her way.

"What my grandmother lacked in cash, she made up for in an abundance of dreams. She had an unrelenting belief in me, greater than any belief I held about myself. No matter the circumstances or challenges, she was determined that I would go places in life that she and my mother had only dreamed about. Every woman should have a blue-haired lady like my grandmother in her life. She is the woman who thinks you are terrific even when you don't feel terrific—the woman who always believes that anything is possible, no matter the odds.

"Thanks to her, I attended college, landed an exciting corporate job, and made more money in a year than my mother had made in ten. Years later, I co-founded a management consulting firm, wrote six books, and gave speeches all over the world. Consulting with leaders (including a US President), I had the opportunity to work with some of America's most powerful people in a world that had been closed to my grandmother. Yet she was my inspiration."

Obstacles and Possibilities

"Obstacles and possibilities often meld together to form defining moments in life, sometimes appearing just when we think we have life figured out. Unfortunately, smartly compartmentalized lives can be turned upside down in a matter of moments. One such moment involved my husband, Mike. After playing a round of golf, he experienced waves of pain that made him unable to walk as muscles spasmed throughout his body. After six months and numerous trips to the University of California-San Francisco Medical Center, doctors began to unravel the illness that was ravaging his body, which, by that time, had destroyed over half his lung capacity. His diagnosis began with the term "pulmonary fibrosis, caused by dermatomyositis and polymyositis"— words I could neither pronounce nor understand. We were told that he had five to six years to live. Our children were ages six and ten. The doctors suggested a lung transplant.

"Writing on Memorial Day, a time when we honor those who have served and died in wars, I realize that my husband was a veteran of a very different kind of war—a war on a rare disease. It is twelve years since his diagnosis and three and a half years since his death. Mike outlived his doctors' prognosis by so many years that he was among the longest living patients ever treated for pulmonary fibrosis. When he died, Jackie remembered this warrior by having the American flag flown at half staff on the nation's capital in his honor.

"Mike and I and our children spent over half our lives fighting this terrible disease while trying to live a normal life. There were times of fear and sadness and many times of happiness. There were battles with insurance companies over experimental drugs, prior authorizations, and responsible parties. There were hospitalizations and ambulance rides in the middle of the night. There was a move from our home in San Francisco to a small Midwestern town—a move that brought us closer to Mike's family and acknowledged the reality that the lung transplant list in that region was shorter.

Many women have stories like mine. The difference? I am blessed with friends like Jackie, Jan, and Michealene, and I am supported by the wisdom of other women that helped prepare me for a future I didn't want.

"Moving to a small community in the Midwest at the age of fifty meant leaving behind my home, friends I loved, and a support system that I had always relied upon. I carried a piece of paper in my purse for courage that read: What would the blue-haired lady do? While I didn't know a single woman in my new state, however, I knew the importance of women's friendships in my life. So I tried to figure out how to meet as many women as I could in the shortest period of time. My solution was to create a women's conference similar to the one Jackie had started in California. Today, that conference is in its eighth year and has grown to be the largest event of its kind for women in the Midwest.

"Billie Dragoo, now my closest friend in my new home, joined me in getting the conference off the ground. After meeting her for coffee one morning, I knew she was the kind of person every woman should have in her corner. She opened up doors for me, introduced me to others, and was encouraging and kind.

"I tackled my husband's illness, our move, and our family's transition as my most important project. I followed the steps and the advice given in this book almost as a textbook case. Yet as Mike's disease progressed, I never once thought about what my life would be like after his death. Planning for a future without him never registered in my thoughts."

Light Travels Through Broken Places

"A strong voice inside spoke to me on many sleepless nights. It said that my obligation was to help my husband die with dignity. Gail Sheehy, author of the iconic book *Passages,* had traveled a similar journey with her husband and she introduced me to hospice and palliative care when she spoke at my conference. I'll always be grateful for her caring advice.

I set up a meeting with Mike's doctor and broached the subject of hospice. He agreed and gently told Mike that he needed to get his affairs in order.

"Mike, still determined to fight his illness, struggled to accept his reality. 'After you have fought so hard for so many years and battled the odds, it is difficult to turn off the fight,' he said. As primary caregiver, I spent most of my time at home, which now resembled a hospital. I was extremely grateful that I was able to care for Mike, but I quickly learned how lonely and scary caregiving can be.

"I was still working—I had to work, as we had enormous medical bills. We were extremely lucky to have escaped bankruptcy. In fact, over 60 percent of families dealing with a terminal illness go broke and far too many women lose their homes and any sense of security when a spouse dies. The whole process is akin to landing a 747 in the midst of a war zone.

"I quickly learned how to compartmentalize, going to the upstairs bedroom to conduct conference calls for my work while knowing that one floor below, my husband lay in a bed dying. Trying to be 'normal' while living in the most abnormal and heart-breaking of circumstances was excruciating. Michealene described perfectly how I felt—like an old thermos bottle encasing shattered glass. The thermos looked perfectly normal on the outside, but when it moved, you could hear the tinkle of the shattered pieces. That was me.

"My friend, Billie, introduced me to Dr. B., a psychiatrist who met with me weekly to help us through Mike's nine-month hospice journey. More coach than psychiatrist, Dr. B. overflowed with life wisdom. He gave me assignments each week, all crafted to help us through difficult moments. One in particular made an amazing difference. He asked me what I thought of when I heard circus music. I responded: Happy, cheerful, smiling kids, lighthearted. He instructed me to download as much circus music onto my computer as possible and to start playing it at home. What sounded crazy at the time turned out to be nothing short of remarkable.

The music took our minds to a joyful place that made the moments easier to handle. My husband got the biggest smile on his face whenever he heard it. Today, that is the face I remember—that big smile. If you're lucky, you get to engage with a remarkable human being like Dr. B. His lessons will accompany me forever."

This Isn't My First Rodeo

"Sheryl, the hospice nurse who cared for Mike, had spent twenty-five years tending to the dying. I'm convinced that the blue-haired lady sent her to us. Sheryl's favorite saying was: 'Deborah, this isn't my first rodeo and I hope you'll learn to trust me. I'm going to be with you every step of the way.' Sheryl counseled me to live through this time with no regrets, and taught me that living with no regrets meant savoring the day, the hour, the moment. It meant letting no words pass through my lips that I would regret after Mike's death. When you live with someone who is dying, even the most mundane of days become important. You wonder: Is this the last minute? The last hour? The last day? The times are so stressful and heart-breaking and funny and memorable and devastating.

DEBORAH CHECKED AGAIN, BUT THERE WERE NO EASY ANSWERS.

"Sheryl believed that people die in much the same way they have lived. Her words were true for Mike, as he refused to see death as a possibility. This admirable quality served him well in the fight against his disease. Yet now, facing death, that trait caused chaos, along with physical and emotional pain that seeped into all our lives. We undertook the task of encouraging Mike to surrender to his illness. Our children, Aaron and Lily, took on roles no children should ever have to fill. They sat with their dad, the hospice team, and the priest, and asked him to quit fighting. They gave him permission to die. Several weeks later, Mike's last words to me were: 'You are so beautiful. I love you. Let's go home.'"

Endings

Three months after the death of her husband, Deborah's mother was hospitalized, diagnosed with congestive heart failure, and placed in a nursing home. Several weeks later, her sister-in-law was diagnosed with leukemia and undertook a stem-cell transplant and more rounds of chemotherapy than she believed any person could survive. "My husband had died; my sister-in-law had died; and my mother was close to dying. My mind and body—but above all, my soul—were depleted.

"I recall Jackie and Jan describing grief as being on the beach while waves come crashing down upon you with little warning. Death changes everything. Well-meaning friends, even your own family members, want you to be 'okay' as fast as is humanly possible. Each time they look into your eyes, you bring home to them the reality of endings and it's often uncomfortable. Endings impact our children no matter how hard we try to protect them. I am blessed. My children are remarkably kind, healthy, and well-adjusted adults. Due to their life experiences, they carry a wisdom and resilience that most their ages do not. Aaron is a global product manager for a medical-device company. Lily is an account executive for a medical-device company and Mairi is a nurse. My children, my co-authors, a few close friends, and an extraordinary hospice team have helped me in countless ways.

"It is true what Ram Dass states: 'We are all just walking each other home.'"

6
WHEN YOU ARE STANDING AT THE EDGE OF THE POOL, JUMP IN.

I read and walked for miles at night along the beach, writing bad verse and searching endlessly for someone wonderful who would step out of the darkness and change my life. It never crossed my mind that person could be me.

ANNA QUINDLEN, WRITER (1952–)

Hide-and-Seek

"As a child, and into adulthood, I learned to hide my light from others so that no one would hurt me. Perhaps it came from being sexually abused and learning that people can take very special parts of you without your permission. As a result, I developed a fear that someone would take that very special part of me and destroy it. I am Michealene Christini Risley and I became an expert at hide-and-seek.

"I hid my talents because I did not want people to notice and hurt me or take away those gifts. I worked my way through life, getting close to all of the things that I dreamed of—but never having them. In my career, I took jobs that circled around my dreams. I stared longingly from the sidelines, hoping for what seemed so far out of reach. The experience was like having your swimsuit on at the edge of the pool, but never having the courage to jump in. I secretly hoped that someone would grab my hand and help me into the water.

"What I needed most was for someone to tell me that it was okay to want those things—it was okay to dream and be—and that I wasn't a child anymore. My fantasy was always that this person would nurture my talents, while protecting me. My own inner voices were hard to conquer. How dare I hope for things in my life? How dare I dream so large? Friends and family looked at my career and marveled at how happy and successful I was. I was the only one who knew the truth—that I was still standing at the edge of the pool waiting to jump in.

"I gave birth to our first child the same day that my father had a brain tumor removed. Life and death seem always to be intertwined. I didn't know if Dad would make it out of surgery alive, but I had to try to find a way to celebrate the gift of a healthy baby boy. These moments were bittersweet.

"Weeks later, I traveled to visit my father in the hospital and he got to see his eleventh grandson. I studied his face as it lit up with joy at his first glimpse of my son. But as I spent time with him in the ICU, it dawned on me that my dad's life would end soon.

"I stood at the foot of the hospital bed as he turned to me and called out a name—Mary Jane, the name of my childhood friend. I froze, as I had spent years rehearsing this conversation. I had always wanted to confront my father, but somehow I came to believe growing up that, if you told your parents bad things, it would cause their death. It was a difficult belief to hold inside a family full of secrets. Could this possibly be the right moment? Not now, not when he was dying. Yet, *he* was trying to talk about it. I wanted to run for the nearest exit.

"Standing in the ICU, I felt transported back in time. There was the puke-green tile that framed the mirror on the kitchen wall. I could hear the crackle of the olive oil heating up in the frying pan. Terror engulfed me as I approached my mother, who stood with her hands deep in the sudsy sink and her back to me. She whirled around as I said: 'Mom, Mary Jane says Dad put his hand down her pants.'"

A Family Full of Secrets

"My mother exploded with all the rage of an erupting volcano. How could I ever think that my father would do something like that? How could I think that? What was wrong with me? But if Mom could not believe what Dad had done to Mary Jane, how could she ever believe what he had done to me? I felt numb.

"The memories of those moments in the kitchen seared into my mind as I stood at the foot of my father's deathbed. Did I have the courage? Did he have the strength? Was this fair for me to do this now, or ever? Here was my chance, and I had become that young girl again, waiting for someone to take my hand, unable to string two coherent words together. The opportunity passed.

"We took time to say good-bye. Even though Dad was in a coma, the nurses told us he would be able to hear until the end. When it was my turn, I curled up on the bed next to him and whispered: 'Dad, we both made mistakes, and I am sorry for that. I forgive you.' I felt the tension leave his body.

"In stark clarity during that moment, I realized that I was no longer that abused child. My choice to hide myself, into adulthood, made me into an abuser—of myself. Through my father's death and becoming a mother, I realized that those events that had happened in the past no longer defined who I was or how much I deserved in life. Enough. In that moment, I broke free of the past and fully jumped into my life without fear.

"When our book was published, it caused great anguish in my family. My mother cried, two brothers stopped speaking to me, and one died from a heart attack during that period. An uncle was convinced I had lied to sell books. It was painful. Yet, my sisters always supported me. They never waivered.

"The publication of our book cleared a path for my mother and me to talk through the events of my childhood, and the wedge between us disintegrated. When she asked why I hadn't told her, her words melted away my resentment at not being heard and our relationship deepened until her death. She was a beautiful, loving mother and friend with an impish sense of humor.

Where in the World Is Zimbabwe?

"Challenges did not end for me. I had emergency spinal surgery and was adjusting to being a mom to three young, active boys, hoping that my life would slow down. Then I met Paola Gianturco.

"Paola traveled as a photojournalist and had published six books documenting women's lives all over the world. We often met for coffee or dinner, where she shared her amazing stories about young girls—and in particular, girls from Africa. One of these stories was about Betty Makoni and the Girl Child Network in Zimbabwe. There was a myth propagated in Africa that, if AIDS-infected men raped virgins, it would rid them of the deadly virus. Betty worked to rescue these girls and help them to rebuild their lives. Paola suggested that I visit Zimbabwe to film their stories.

"When we went to hear Betty Makoni speak in San Francisco, I brought along some copies of my first film, which focused on child sexual abuse in America. The film had won awards, was screened at the Cannes Film Festival, and had been aired on PBS. Betty accepted my gift as if those films were the most precious of things. She understood. Her commitment to these kids fed my soul, and I left that breakfast promising to visit Zimbabwe and to tell the story of the Girl Child Network.

"I hurried home to my computer and typed in the search string 'Where in the world is Zimbabwe?' After gleaning as much information as I could, my assistant, Lauren Carara, and I prepared to make our way across the world to Harare, the capital of Zimbabwe. Although I had traveled extensively, nothing prepared me for the devastation we saw there. Robert Mugabe, the nation's dictator, had seized and forcibly redistributed most of the country's commercial farms to political allies, most of whom had no idea how to farm. People were restless and suffering under severe water

THIS IS NOT THE LIFE I ORDERED

and food shortages. Unemployment was at 80 percent and life expectancy had decreased significantly.

"When we were stopped by the Central Intelligence Organization on our first day, I recalled my husband's parting words: 'Would you feel the trip to have been worth it if you didn't come back?' I didn't take him too seriously at the time, as I thought he was exaggerating the dangers. It dawned on me on that day, however, that he might have been right.

"Although I had worked all my professional life with poverty, I had never gone hungry. But everywhere I looked in Africa, hunger smacked me awake. One day, while with Betty in the Girl Child Village, an elderly grandmother arrived with a young boy and girl. The three of them had walked for days searching for food. While we washed for dinner, I heard bits and pieces of their story and knew that they were starving. The children were placed on the grass to my left and sat waiting. The administrator explained to me that custom in Zimbabwe requires that elders be served first, then adults, and finally children. The children sat looking at the food on our plates. I quickly lost my appetite and still today am haunted by those images and the children's hunger.

"One morning, while staying at Betty's house, I was craving an American breakfast and I asked Johannes, our bodyguard, to take us to eat. When we arrived back at the compound, the guard who usually sat at the gate was gone. Johannes leaned back and said to us: 'Something is wrong; stay in the car.' We had spent the last week with this man and felt as if we had come to know him. His face said it all. Something was terribly, terribly wrong.

"The gate flew open and fifteen very large African men quickly surrounded the car. Johannes came running out from among them and jumped into the driver's seat. He drove frantically through the gate and pulled to the side of the house. We exited the car and were immediately surrounded by a group of Zimbabweans who were shouting and brandishing guns. I was scared. One of the leaders started peppering me with questions about our camera and asked if I was an agent for the CIA.

"It was chaos as they took us into the house and searched our suitcases. We were transported to a Zimbabwean prison that was renowned for torture where we spent three harrowing days in an overcrowded building without food or water and with no protection from anyone. I witnessed someone forced to have sex, and saw a young man tortured. The gaping holes in the ceiling forced us to dodge feces and urine from those imprisoned above us. We bribed our way into another cell—a five-foot-by-eight-foot room that housed eight women. It had no windows, just a wooden door, and contained nothing but a small bench.

"On the bench lay a young woman who kept coughing up blood. Another woman had been badly beaten by her husband. Most of the women had been incarcerated for 'border jumping' in an effort to get food for their children. They told of risking rape and crocodiles to feed their families—of getting thrown into prison and released, and then starting all over again. About halfway through their stories, I began to weep. The woman who seemed to be the leader of the group asked why I was crying. I replied: 'I cry for you and your lives.' She looked at me with a blank expression, with no apparent comprehension of how little they had, and said: 'It is okay; it is our lives. We will be okay.' But I knew they wouldn't be, and that there was nothing they could do to help themselves. The worst part for them was thinking of their children alone, without adult assistance.

"I felt incredibly guilty about getting Lauren involved in my work, and I kept thinking about my husband and the boys. I had come to work on issues for women and children, never realizing that I might leave my own children without a mother. I felt overwhelming despair and was inconsolable. How could I risk my boys not having their mother to raise them? I went from thinking that I was building awareness about an awful practice in Zimbabwe to feeling incredible shame for my choices. How could I have been so selfish?"

"When he learned of our predicament, my husband hired a human rights lawyer. The US embassy intervened and a man I had met on Facebook called his friend at the CIA. Their combined efforts led to our release and deportation.

"My imprisonment impacted my family. When Lauren and I left for Zimbabwe, Christopher was eleven, Austin was nine, and Dillon was four. When we finally arrived home and could tell the kids what had happened, I found that they reacted in different ways. Christopher, always practical, said: 'Mom I hear that you can't go back to Africa anymore.' Austin was just glad to have me back. But, the impact on Dillon would not become apparent until a few years later.

"My life changed after Africa. The experience opened my eyes to images I can never un-see and memories I can never un-remember. I continue to be blessed by a happy marriage and our three boys are rapidly growing into young men. I am proof that we can face our demons, endure hardships, and go on to create great lives."

7
LISTEN TO THE CHILDREN.

Sometimes when I need a miracle, I look into my children's eyes and realize I've already created miracles.

ANN LANDERS, AMERICAN AUTHOR (1918–2002)

Minus One at the Dinner Table

As we each worked to create environments filled with joy even in the worst of circumstances, we tried to protect our children. Unfortunately, death and grief and loss have a way of affecting every aspect of a child's life. Conversations around the dinner table are minus one. There are soccer practices, ballgames and recitals, parent-teacher conferences, graduations, and marriages where what's missing is felt by all involved. Children carry around fears that they often hold inside and don't share. We, as mothers, carry around guilt that we haven't done enough to help them through the dark times.

When we began meeting around the kitchen table, all our children were quite young. Today, most of them are adults. We are so very happy to tell you that the kids are all right! Since each of them has traveled with us on this journey, we thought that the "wisdom coming from the mouth of our babes" might be helpful to others as well. So we asked them several questions about their experiences. What follows are reflections and advice from some (not all) of them.

If It's Worth Doing, It's Worth Overdoing

Jan's daughter Jenna was ten when her dad died. She is now thirty-three. Jenna worked in New York for ten years producing shows for the Food Network. She is married, lives in Los Angeles, and has her own production company. She also writes *The Pickle* (*readthepickle.com*), a website about food—what and when to eat, where to buy, and how to enjoy and share. Please do subscribe; it's free!

Jenna thinks the biggest challenge she experienced when her dad died was learning how to understand his death. She tells how a well-meaning therapist told her she wouldn't understand it until she got older. "Adults, do not say things like this to children," says Jenna. "It comes across as patronizing and only made me want to prove the therapist wrong. At ten, of course, I didn't understand the full scope of how losing my dad would affect me. But then, do any of us at any age fully understand it when a tragedy rocks our world?

"Wanting to prove the therapist wrong resulted in me avoiding talking about my father's death, and my feelings surrounding it. I put on a brave face and acted strong, as if I had my grief under control and didn't need any help or special treatment. But grieving, I learned over the years, cannot be controlled, cannot be suppressed, and cannot be rushed. We all deal with tragedy in our own way, and that usually does evolve over time. But grieve we must. It has helped me immensely to lean on family, friends, and trained professionals. I learned that, while painful and clumsy at first, opening up and sharing my feelings was the only way I could heal.

"It was difficult for me, my siblings, and our mom to face the future without Daddy. Who would dance with me at the sixth-grade father-daughter Cotillion? I'd looked forward to that dance for two years, ever since he took my older sister. What would Father's Day look like? What would we do on Thanksgiving without my dad entertaining friends and family with his famous annual feast?

"Who would walk me down the aisle at my wedding?

"A father's role in his daughter's wedding is traditionally significant, even to a young girl. Within the year after my dad died, I remember my mom saying to me that her brother, my Uncle Derick, could walk me down the aisle when the day came. I can't remember why it came up—if I asked, or if my mom offered—but I've never forgotten that conversation. I've always been close to my Uncle Derick, but when my husband, John, proposed, there was no question in my mind: My mom would be the one to walk me down the aisle. When I married the man of my dreams, that is exactly what happened."

The wedding was everything Jenna could have wanted— great food, great music, dancing, and, of course, her nearest and dearest in attendance. John and his family processed in, followed by her siblings. Then she entered, arm-in-arm with Jan. "We walked to *Here Comes the Sun*, from the Beatles' vinyl album that I inherited from my dad's record collection. We were ten steps down the aisle when I looked over and saw my mom's eyes welling up with tears. I held her a little bit tighter, feeling her joy and pride. I didn't sense sadness in her and, as I think about it now, I didn't feel sadness either.

"You might expect that I would have felt great sadness that my dad wasn't with me on this special day. But I had made sure that he *would* be there. When I arrived at the altar, there he was, dressed in a sweet Eighties tux, beaming at me from a crisp white picture frame positioned on a front-row seat. It was important to me to have a photo of my dad there for two reasons," Jenna recalls fondly, "to honor him before our wedding guests (many of whom had known and loved him), and to make sure that I saw his bright smile as I looked out on all the other guests' faces. I'll never forget the sense of joy and support radiating from our loved ones during the ceremony, and I'm so glad I got to bring my dad into that memory."

Jenna called on him again during what is traditionally the father-daughter dance, boogying with her mom to Tina Turner's *Simply the Best*, which a colleague of her father's had emotionally—and brilliantly—performed at his memorial service. "I was 98 percent positive that song would bring my mom to tears (I had kept it as a surprise). To my own surprise, however, her eyes stayed dry. I think both of us were just *happy*—happy I had found a wonderful partner, happy to be celebrating love, and happy to be surrounded by our friends and family, including my dad.

"They say time heals all wounds," Jenna reflects. "I wouldn't say time has made me whole again—I still miss my dad. I wish he had gotten to know my husband and our future children. I wish I could have heard what he would have told me moments before walking me down the aisle— but time has given me perspective. If I could talk to my Dad today, I, of course, would tell him that I love him. I would also thank him for teaching me how to live."

As Jenna matures into her thirties, she tells us, she still benefits from life advice from her mom—sometimes solicited, sometimes not. It's perhaps a universal impulse for parents to want to download a lifetime of lessons to their children. "I'm willing to bet," Jenna claims, "that at forty-six, my father departed this world feeling as if he hadn't had enough time to teach my siblings and me all the lessons he'd learned over his too-short, but richly lived lifetime." While she admits missing the opportunity to ask her father for advice, she nonetheless carries with her his overall approach to life—one that guides her every day.

"My dad's life motto, which we put on his gravestone, was: If it's worth doing, it's worth overdoing! He didn't just go fishing; he planned epic deep-sea fishing journeys. He didn't just go hiking; he took multi-week treks through jungles stalking giant gorillas, photographing them, and returning to display his images like trophies in huge frames throughout our home. He didn't just take his five- and seven-year-old daughters camping; he took them on a white-water rafting trip with his adult friends.

"My dad loved people, his family, traveling, learning about different cultures, and—oh, yes—he loved laughing. He saw life as one big adventure, embracing it full on. Living with that kind of zest, that kind of presence in the moment, remains a great example that I try to follow in my own life, and that I've similarly seen my siblings embrace. I now find strength in what I know—that my friends and family love me, that my dad loved me, and that he wanted me to live a rich and happy life. So I let friends and family step in where my dad can't, knowing he is cheering me on from his front-row seat."

Sorry to Hear That

Jan's son JB, now thirty, was six when his dad died just ten days shy of his seventh birthday. A month after graduation from the University of Arizona, he moved to "Lala Land." He now lives in Santa Monica, California. It's where he knew he would be happy, as he loves everything about the production of movies and short-form shows. He is also hosting on *After Buzz TV*. JB says: "I was perhaps too young to grasp the impact the loss of my dad would have on my life, but I was also too old to ignore it. Ultimately, I think that losing my father at such a young age may have made it easier to accept the reality of the loss in my own mind. I never questioned his passing; I questioned everyone else.

"Growing up, the toughest part for me was speaking about it. I couldn't share my story with others. Not because it was hard or hurtful—although, of course, it was those things—but the pain was in the background. For me, admitting it aloud felt almost like telling someone about a weakness. It was awkward, discouraging, and depressing. I never tried to hide my story, but it was uncomfortable, as it brought about such a somber switch in every situation. The very mention of Dad's death opened the same deluge of sorrow and pity from everyone around me. It sounds weird to complain about, but, as a child being surrounded by sadness at a time when even throwing rocks is fun, it felt like something to avoid."

JB never blamed anyone for offering him words of comfort, he recalls. "I think people innately want to offer sympathy, which is a great thing. I just never let those assurances do their duty. I never let them help. I got hung up on the phrase people say to you: 'Sorry to hear that.' I was perplexed and questioned why strangers would be sorry when they did nothing to cause harm. My mind accepted my dad's passing. It was just that my heart did not. It was only recently, in the back half of my twenties, that I tried to look beyond the word 'sorry' itself and hear the support underneath. What everyone was really saying was: That sucks. And they are not wrong. I only wish I had been able to translate that earlier."

JB's advice is simple: Don't feel *different*. "You are not," he claims. "And that's a good thing. While your own tragedy may have affected you in a certain way, everyone deals with death. Everyone deals with difficulty. You are not *different* from other people because of your suffering. You are *special*. Special because you're alive. Special because you survived it. Special because you experienced something that terrifies everyone on earth and you came out the other side. Special because now you can share that with the world.

"No doubt the horrific experience will influence you. You went through an extraordinarily devastating event. It has to impact you, but it doesn't have to define you. You can define it. You can use it to grow.

"People will try to give you empathy. Embrace it. Embrace them. People will try to underestimate you. Let them. Then achieve beyond their expectations. You can only become better if you try to be. So try. Fail. Try again. Repeat until you're happy. Life rains on everyone; don't wait outside in the cold. Find warmth. Find happiness. Find love. Find laughter. Find everything you want in this world today, not tomorrow.

"Also, smile—people like that."

JB has always believed the spirit of his dad lives within him. "So I feel as if he already knows everything about me. I often keep him in my thoughts, surfacing his presence in my consciousness at times when I think he'd be proud. At other times, I turn to him when I am making drastic decisions— his acumen for financial responsibility making appearances more recently—and as a silent sounding board."

Although JB doesn't think there's much he needs to tell his dad, he admits that there's an infinite number of things he wants to ask him. "I'd ask him *everything*. I know who my dad was. I've met him. I've heard the flattering, funny, and fantastic stories about him from everyone that knew him throughout his life (including his parents). I remember his love of poker, fishing, and, of course, his bright red Acura NSX. But who would he be to me now?

"Now that I've grown up, what treasure trove of truths would he reveal to me alone as an adult. What stories did he save? What jokes? What wild, crazy, secret shenanigans from his past would he reveal now that I'm old enough to hear them? If I could understand him as a friend as well as a father, what would he admit he wants to learn? What did he regret? What scared the shit out of him? What rushed through his mind the moment he met my mom?

"I'd ask him what only he could tell me. I'd ask him what only he knew. I'd get to know the man he'd only be with me. I'd listen. I'd learn. I'd laugh. A lot."

Not Gone—Just on a Long Vacation

Jan's eldest daughter, Jaclyn, is now thirty-six. She was twelve when her dad died. She has worked for US Senator Mazie Hirono (D-Hawaii) in Washington, DC, and for an international bank in London. She has owned a wine shop and is now a sommelier for an upscale restaurant in her adopted city of Berlin, Germany.

Jaclyn recalls that losing her dad at twelve was very hard. In fact, she found it very difficult to comprehend his passing at the time. "I constantly felt as if he were on vacation—that he would return at any moment to give me a giant bear hug. At the time, I knew I had to step up, be more helpful, and be more dependable; I was proud of myself that I was able to be so mature.

"I think the toughest part was years later, in college, when I truly noticed the magnitude of losing my dad so early. I was trying to find myself and figure out my interests, strengths, weaknesses, and goals for life. I realized how valuable it would have been to sit down with him and ask for his advice, his support, his accounting wisdom, and his strategic guidance on how I could become a successful businesswoman."

The loss of a parent or loved one is painful, difficult, and heartbreaking. Surrounding yourself with family, friends, and loved ones is essential for the grieving process, for surviving your loss, and for figuring out how life moves on. "You are not defined by your loss," Jaclyn maintains, "and you are not alone. Sometimes you will want to talk about it and sometimes you won't—both options are normal. My best advice is to remember to be thankful. Be thankful for the people in your life who love you. Be thankful for the good times you had with your loved one, and remember those times. Often. The importance of that person in your life stays with you, in your heart, forever.

"If I were able, I would tell my dad thank you and I love you. Thank you for teaching me to enjoy life to the absolute fullest. I adopted your big laugh, your love of life and adventure, and your penchant for risk-taking. Thank you for being there to support me every step of the way."

Why Don't We Have a Daddy?

Jackie's daughter Stephanie Sierra is twenty-three and is a broadcast journalist in Colorado. Jackie was three months pregnant with Stephanie when her father, Steve Sierra, was killed in a horrific car crash. She was named in honor of the father she never knew.

Stephanie says: "Growing up as a young kid in my family was an adventure. From princess-sparkly birthday parties to running around at Chucky Cheese, life with mom, Jackson, and myself was perfect. I didn't know it could be any better."

By the time she reached the age of five, however, embarking on her first day at kindergarten, she started to realize that not all families came in groups of three. "After school," she recalls, "I saw fathers waiting to pick up their daughters and mothers doing the same. School lunch hour was filled with stories of my classmates planning play dates and discussing what group would be performing at the school talent show. It didn't dawn on me until the ripe old age of six that most of my friends had a man in the house they called 'Dad.' At that age, I was too young to understand what had happened to my father, so I simply didn't know to ask about it.

"It didn't faze me as a young child. I was the happiest 'little munchkin,' as my mom called me. I was old enough to realize that my mom worked hard. Jackson and I had Christine, our live-in nanny. Christine did a lot for us, but I will never forget anxiously waiting for mom to come home every night. Looking back on it now, she was incredibly dedicated, putting up with a rigorous schedule of driving four-plus hours everyday just so she could be home with Jackson and me every night."

Stephanie remembers having the closest relationship a mother and daughter could have—then and now. "She was my best friend then and my best friend now," she claims. "And I will never forget the 'talk.' It's hard to remember a lot of things that happened over ten years ago, but I will never forget the day I asked Mom: 'Why don't we have a daddy? All my friends do.' I asked this as an inquisitive seven-year-old, but later would have bitten my tongue rather than bring that up, because mom's infamous dating era began a year later!

"I hated it. I wanted her all to myself. I was selfish in that way. Given how close we were, I didn't like that she was going on what seemed like random dates with men I'd never met before. My brother Jackson and I joked about some of them we didn't like. One we nicknamed Psycho Doc because every time they went on a running date, one of us would answer the door to find him just running on the doorstep!"

Shortly after that, Jackie went on a date with a man named Barry Dennis. And Barry lasted a lot longer than the others. "Barry was very nice," Stephanie remembers. "Down to earth, a fisherman, and he made us the most delicious pork chops. I always loved seeing Mom so happy after spending time with him. And then before I knew it—there was a wedding!

"I quickly learned how blessed Jackson and I were to have such a dedicated, loyal, and loving man in our lives. Barry later adopted us as his own children, making him our dad. And there we were—a happy family of four."

Choose Your Own Path

Jackie's son, Jackson Sierra, is twenty-nine. He was five years old when his father was killed in that horrible car crash. After he graduated from Stanford, he began work as a software engineer in Silicon Valley. Jackson describes the difficulty he had differentiating his own feelings as a child from the recollections of others who had lost a parent. As a young child, he admits, he understandably failed to appreciate the gravity of the moment and just continued on with his daily routine, only finding out much later the moment he had let pass by. "Such was my experience," he recalls, "a few fleeting memories with my dad and life almost beginning thereafter."

The experience subtly nudged Jackson toward independence, however, making him an individual with the confidence to take on most challenges, yet quite reserved in asking for help from family and friends. "Perhaps having a dad around during those formative years might have given me different perspectives and experiences that would have balanced my fierce individualism. But while I may have missed the advice I never had from my father, I had a strong, loving mother who more than made up the difference.

"There's a notion today that a young child will follow in a fallen parent's footsteps—by trying out for the same sports team, or attending the same alma mater, or pursuing the same career," says Jackson. "But we're also fortunate to live in a society that allows us to choose our own paths, to be ourselves, without being saddled with the burden of expectations. That's not to say that you shouldn't strive for the same goals as your parents. You can, but charting your own course is just as acceptable."

Jackson notes that a great testament to someone's life is how fondly and frequently they're remembered by those who were close to them. "Certainly we'd all be happy to know that we're viewed in a positive light when brought up in conversation. But what separates my dad from others," he remarks, "is how his existence, his being, and the way he enriched people's lives is something that those who knew him can talk about and lose track of time. The stories go on and on. And before you know it, the restaurant is empty, or the early-evening dinner party has extended into the next day. People love stories in part because they arouse their feelings. And my dad was one of the best in eliciting feelings from just about anyone."

Always Rise

Lily Stephens is Deborah's daughter. She is twenty-six, and was twenty-two when her dad died. She works in the medical-device industry in Colorado. Her dad became ill when Lily was in elementary school and died during her last year of college. Through all the health emergencies and hospitalizations, Lily knew that her family was different, but she remembers that her dad had a very convincing way of making everything seem normal. She never believed that her father would die—and that's the way the family lived. She describes her dad as "the comeback king" and remembers a particular song he used to play really loudly, encouraging her brother and her to sing it with him: "I get knocked down; I get up again. I get knocked down, but nothing's going to keep me down."

"That is how my dad lived," Lily recalls. "Even though he was told that he was dying, he refused to wallow in it or allow me or anyone to be distraught. He spent every day, every minute, doing something, taking some sort of action. And he usually had a smile on his face. I often wondered how he could still smile, still joke with me, still laugh. That he was able to do so during the last months of his life gives me great inspiration. I was fortunate in that my dad spent a lot of time with me. I remember watching my favorite television program (*Say Yes to the Dress*) with him. One day, I was so sad that I asked him who would walk me down the aisle. He responded: 'Honey, I think you are way too far in the future. You need to have a boyfriend before you think about getting married!'"

During her last year in college, Lily trained for eight months for a collegiate bike race. "I really had never worked harder at anything," she reports. "A month before the race, I was diagnosed with mononucleosis and ordered to strict bed rest. The doctor told me that the bike race was not something I could participate in. I was devastated. My dad kept telling me not to give up, but to get healthy. Unbeknownst to my mom, we plotted a way for me to ride in the race. Two weeks before, the doctor cleared me medically, but advised against me riding. My dad, after speaking with the doctor on the health risks, surmised that the risks were small enough that I should just go for it! He believed that, sometimes in life, you just have to take a calculated risk. I finished second in the race and experienced an exhilarating sense of accomplishment. I think my dad knew that this was a life lesson he wanted to imprint on me before he died."

On the day that Lily's dad died, an ambulance was called to take him to the hospice facility, as they could not get his pain under control at home. "He refused to be transported from our house on a stretcher," she recalls. "He put on his hat, told my mom to get him a change of clothes and, before we knew it, he was walking out of the house on his own without a walker or any other support. I think he did it so we would remember him in that way—always getting back up in life and continuing to move forward."

Lily's advice to others who may be going through similar issues is to take advantage of as much help and as many resources as possible—and to do it as early as possible. "I didn't do that right away," she admits. "But about six months after my dad's death, the loss really brought me to my knees. I was so sad and miserable. My mom and brother and the hospice grief counselor helped me through the rough spots. I learned to talk about my feelings and to understand that they were normal. I also thought a great deal about the lessons Dad had left me with. I chose to think of them when grief visited and it helped a lot.

"Today, I would tell my dad that I am so thankful for the impact he had on my life. I got a double dose of tenacity, persistence, and optimism from that gene pool. He will always be with me. I love you, Dad, and I thank you."

I'll Be There

Michealene's kids are still too young to contribute their voices. Her oldest son, Christopher, is at Northeastern in Boston. Austin just finished his first year at Michigan State. And Dillon just finished his first year of high school. "There's so much of my life that they don't understand or know about yet," she says. "But when they are ready, I will be there to explain."

WIT KIT TOOLS FOR MANAGING MISFORTUNE

1. Find a journal and label it My WIT Kit. Now grab a favorite pen, open to the first page, and write down three things you want to experience or accomplish in your lifetime. You may be thinking that, right now, you just want to get through the day. We understand. But this

is your place to dream, your opportunity to think big. In your WIT Kit journal, you have the freedom to look ahead instead of being bogged down in the present. Please don't censor yourself. You can be as frivolous or as idealistic as you like.

2. What one thing can you do this week to make progress on one of those three dreams? If you want to go back to college, pick up the phone and ask your local college to mail you registration requirements and a course catalog. If you want to travel to Europe, go online and check out available deals. If you want to ride horses, visit a local stable and ask about their lessons or trail rides. Just take some active steps! No matter how overwhelmed you are right now, doing one thing to make progress on those three dreams will help move you out of any depressing mood. Once a week, review your three dreams and the actions you have taken. Report in to your kitchen-table group.

3. Get into the habit of writing in your WIT Kit journal every day, even if you only scribble a few lines. It's easiest to make it a habit if you choose a time of day to write—perhaps while sipping your morning tea or for ten minutes before bed. Believe us—this investment will pay off for you in many ways. Your WIT Kit journal is a place to express yourself so that you don't bottle up emotions. You will be able to note progress and have a visible record of where you are now and where you were a short while ago.

CHAPTER TWO

LEARNING TO LOVE MISTAKES

Making a damn fool of yourself is absolutely essential. So, whatever you want to do, just do it. Don't be stifled by the fear of a good mistake.

**GLORIA STEINEM,
ACTIVIST AND WRITER (1934–)**

8
BE WILLING TO MAKE
GREAT MISTAKES.

Mistakes are a part of the dues one pays for a full life.

SOPHIA LOREN, ITALIAN ACTRESS (1934–)

Smart people learn as much, if not more, from mistakes as they do from successes. Mistakes in scientific laboratories have resulted in life-changing inventions like penicillin, microwave ovens, chocolate chip cookies, and Botox. In our own lives, success has often been the artful management of our "creative mistakes."

Research shows that men recover from their mistakes faster than women. Perhaps it's because women are often penalized more heavily by society for their mistakes. Laura Liswood, former Secretary General of the United Nations Council on Women, interviewed thirteen women who were serving as heads of state. All thirteen agreed that society does not tolerate women's mistakes as easily as it does men's. When you hear commentary like that from women who are leading nations, it doesn't take a rocket scientist to figure out why some women fear making mistakes!

Yet we must not fear our mistakes. So when we were asked to speak at a women's conference on a topic of our choice, Jan suggested that we speak about our "best mistakes." She reasoned that we ought to start encouraging women to bring their mistakes out of hidden spaces by shining a light onto their "oops" moments.

The day of the conference, we were shocked when more than 600 women showed up to participate. The workshop was so successful that we were asked to repeat it at the California Governor's Conference on Women that same year. It was a rather humbling endeavor for us to recount our mistakes in public. But it was also very liberating. Our voices gave the women in the audience permission to celebrate their own mistakes and turn the lessons into wisdom.

Creative Accidents

Sitting in the faculty club at Stanford University, the four of us were surrounded by photographs of Nobel Prize winners and presidents as we awaited the arrival of Sara Little Turnbull—the Mother of Invention.

For thirty years, Sara was an influential consultant to dozens of companies—"corporate America's secret weapon" they called her. Sarah joined Stanford's graduate business and engineering schools and, for eighteen years, taught hands-on seminars. "I see design as essentially creating order," Sara told us. "But I also encourage students to learn to let their minds meander to discover the unexpected and the creative accidents." Sara told us that creative accidents hold the seeds of greatness.

Sarah has the ability to take what she refers to as her "brink-of-failure designs" and turn them into her life's best work. She is a master of the "creative accident." For Corning, she designed the "classic" Corning Ware—the oven-to-freezer cookware made of ceramic material like that found on spacecraft heat shields. "You have to push forward when you are on the brink of failure," said Sara. "I'm always questioning, always asking why. I don't fear mistakes; I look for them!"

The Theory of "Oops"

Researchers at Vanderbilt University have identified a part of the human brain that becomes very active when we begin to make a mistake. In fact, this "oops center" not only detects when we're about to make an error; it works to prevent it!

We're convinced that women are best equipped to capitalize on their oops centers, because we are more open and willing to share our mistakes with others. Why is sharing important? you ask. Aren't we supposed to downplay our mistakes and exude that confident, poised, "got it all together" routine? Well, yes and no.

After a decade of shelving studies that either failed or ended in negative results, Dr. Bjorn Olsen at Harvard University saw the value in a few good mistakes—in fact, a worldwide collection of mistakes. In 2002, Olsen created the *Journal of Negative Results*, which focuses only on scientific studies that did not work. Now, you might think that Dr. Olsen's approach to science is a little askew. What scientist wants to publish his or her biggest mistakes in a national journal? Surprisingly, thousands did, including many leading researchers tackling HIV, the cure for cancer, and other important work. Why? Scientists view negative outcomes and mistakes as stepping-stones to answers. Science is based on trial and error.

Over time, the four of us have learned to adopt this "scientific approach" to mistakes. Instead of dreading them, hiding them, or being embarrassed by them, we understand that mistakes, especially when shared, are doorways to discovery. In the next stories, we share what we've learned from some of the common mistakes that women make. If you've already made them, at least you'll know you are not alone!

9
GIVE UP THINKING THAT YOU CAN DO IT ALL.

To live is so startling it leaves little time for anything else.

EMILY DICKINSON, POET (1830–1886)

You've Come a Long Way, Baby

Over the past fifty years, we women have acquired the delusional belief that we can do it all. What made us think we could be Superwomen? What made us believe we could shatter the glass ceiling while bouncing babies on our hips, maintaining perfectly immaculate homes, and doing our best to become intelligent and glamorous wives, girlfriends, and partners? Our ground-breaking path of progress is, in truth, comprised of tired women in well-worn shoes!

Too many women have been brainwashed into thinking they can have it all, do it all, and remain sane and serene in the process. We are here to tell you one simple truth: you cannot. We should know—we have all tried it and failed miserably in the process. Among the four of us, we've traded in "have it all" for "have it all at different times." For us, it is simply a much better way to live.

Having it all at different times requires living your life based upon your own set of personal values. Whether you are single, married, a stay-at-home mom, or a mother who works outside the home—it doesn't matter. What matters is that you are a person who meets or exceeds your own values and expectations, not the values and expectations of others. According to this way of thinking, you choose to design your life around what fits best for you and those you care about.

"STRESS? WHAT STRESS?"

Find Fifteen Minutes

Do you take care of everyone but yourself? Is your life stressful? If you're like many women, your answer is "yes" to both questions. Do you carry around a subconscious belief that putting yourself first is a selfish way to live? If you answered "yes" again, it's time to take baby steps toward honoring your own rights and needs instead of everyone else's. Starting today, carve out a minimum of fifteen minutes to call your own in a twenty-four-hour day. Do this even if you have to wake up early in the morning or stay up late at night to find the time. During that time, take a walk, listen to beautiful music, read a novel, or do anything that connects you to the quietness of life. You will be surprised how rejuvenated you can feel, even after only fifteen minutes of solitude.

10
CREATE "TO-DON'T" LISTS.

Death and taxes and childbirth: there is never any
convenient time for any of them.

MARGARET MITCHELL, AUTHOR OF
***GONE WITH THE WIND* (1900–1949)**

Misguided Pride in Multi-Tasking

We women have been taught to take pride in multi-tasking. Deborah describes how, when her children were both toddlers, her routine mirrored that of countless moms: waking at the crack of dawn, filling bottles with formula, packing diaper bags, and heading out the door by 7:00 AM en route to daycare and the office. Her days and nights were filled with laundry, dirty dishes, children's playtime, grocery shopping, cleaning house, and squeezing in time for her husband. Exhaustion was her normal mode of operation.

"I caught a cold," she remembers. "I thought that, if I missed work, there would be too much to catch up on, so I continued my routine, but added another element. Instead of lunch, I took a thirty-minute nap because I felt so poorly. I eventually ended up in the emergency room and was diagnosed with pneumonia. My mistake of taking care of everyone but myself led to many days of missed work, chores that piled up at home, and disruption in the lives of everyone around me. I learned that I needed to start taking care of myself with the same passion I put into caring for others."

Are You on the List?

We take care of our kids, the dog, the cat, our partners, our co-workers, the team, and our in-laws. Look at any woman's to-do list and the word "me" will be conspicuously absent. We don't get enough sleep, even though we need a good eight hours. We eat on the run and cram every minute of every hour with something to do, say, make, or be. Many of us seem to take pride in multi-tasking and we admire people who fill every minute of the day.

Please, enough of this. It's killing us—literally. We have to move ourselves nearer to the top of the list or we won't be in the state of mind or physical shape to take care of ourselves and those who need us the most. Author and management consultant Tom Peters suggests it's time to turn our to-do lists into "to-don't" lists. We agree.

HOW *DOES* SHE DO IT?

We need to remove things from our to-do lists that don't matter, that don't create value, and that don't make a difference. We need to carve out time for the activities that will create meaningful lives and discard the things that won't.

Think about this tomorrow morning when you compile your to-do list. What two things can you take off that really don't have to be done? Maybe you can order take-out after your long day of work instead of fixing a fancy meal. Maybe it's more important to take your children to the park than to mop the floor. Perhaps you can ask someone else to organize the office party instead of doing it all by yourself.

What can you do to turn your to-do list into a "don't-have-to-do" list?

11
NEVER UNDERESTIMATE YOURSELF.

There is only one real sin, and that is to persuade oneself that the second-best is anything but second best.

DORIS LESSING, BRITISH WRITER (1919–2013)

Polite and Waiting for My Turn

Early in her career, Jackie spent hours of wasted time in self-doubt while she consistently underestimated herself. "I struggled at times to hide my self-doubt and to appear strong," she says. "A year after I lost my first run for Congress, I ran against a twenty-year incumbent for a post on the County Board of Supervisors. And I beat him by 18,000 votes." The experience showed her that she could rally people and that they would believe in her and support her.

"Years later in the State Assembly," she recounts, "I continued to make the same mistake of underestimating myself and allowing self-doubt to cloud my vision. I had very strong opinions about gun control, as I knew firsthand the tragedy guns can cause." She was reluctant to carry any legislation on banning assault weapons, however, because she was told by advisors and colleagues that to do so would mean the end of her political career. They warned that the National Rifle Association would come after her and spend millions of dollars to defeat her.

"In a tiny moment of strength, in the midst of all who told me otherwise, I decided to co-author legislation to ban assault weapons in the state of California. While standing at the podium in the legislative chambers, in the midst of debating the toughest anti-gun legislation in the United States, a colleague approached and interrupted me. 'Ms. Speier,' he asked condescendingly, 'have you ever shot an assault weapon?' Obviously, he didn't know of my past. Stunned, I countered: 'No sir, but have you ever been shot at point-blank range by an assault weapon?' There was dead silence in the chamber. 'Well, I have, and that's why we need this legislation.' The bill was passed overwhelmingly, and many television stations throughout the nation reported on the heated exchange. That experience taught me to quit second-guessing myself."

MISGUIDED MUGS

DON'T WORRY, THEY'LL TAKE CARE OF YOU.

IGNORE YOUR INNER VOICE.

TAKE CARE OF EVERYONE BUT YOURSELF.

FEAR MISTAKES.

UNDERESTIMATE YOURSELF.

FEAR CONFRONTATION, AVOID CONFLICT.

NETWORK AND SEEK FRIENDS ONLY WHEN DESPERATE.

THINK YOU CAN DO IT ALL.

TO SUCCEED BE MORE "LIKE A MAN."

COMMON MISTAKES WOMEN MAKE
(AVOID COLLECTING THE WHOLE SET)

THIS IS NOT THE LIFE I ORDERED

Don't Be Your Own Worst Enemy

Jackie admits that she had always had a tendency in the past not to question authority. "I was always too polite; I always waited my turn. And I gave far too much credence to those in power. I watched other people—less capable, less talented—succeed, while I sat in the stands and looked on. We do such a disservice to ourselves and those around us when we are our own worst enemy in this way."

There is a terrible penalty to be paid for not using your talent. Have you let other people talk you out of pursuing something you're good at? Have you bowed to pressure and abandoned a project that was meaningful to you? Our ability to contribute to this world is directly proportional to our conviction that we have something of value to offer. Vow not to be deterred by doubt—whether it's coming from you or from someone around you. No one wins when we underestimate our capabilities. Identify something you strongly believe in, as Jackie did, and resolve that you will work toward making that a reality. Promise that you will move forward with conviction and courage instead of second-guessing yourself. Commit to not being your own worst enemy.

12
DON'T WAIT UNTIL YOU ARE DEPRESSED OR DESPERATE (OR BOTH) TO NETWORK.

The more I traveled, the more I realized that fear makes strangers of people who should be friends.

SHIRLEY MACLAINE, ACTRESS (1934–)

Do You End When a Job Ends?

Anne Robinson built Windham Hill Records into a Grammy-winning multi-national record company. In 1996, she sold the company to BMG and thought that she would continue in the role of CEO. Instead, BMG exercised their option to buy her out.

"The company had been my whole life for twenty-three years," Anne says, "and in one day, it was over. I hid out and was depressed. Running a large company for twenty-three years left me with little time for anyone, not even myself. I realized I was alone. I hadn't made the time to stay connected to my friends when I worked at Windham Hill. I suddenly realized how important those people were to me. I needed to be with people who cared about me."

If your job becomes your entire life and your job ends, you may end up facing job loss and all it entails alone. When we don't have a lot of time, for whatever reason, our women friends are the first ones we stop seeing. Perhaps we think we can count on them to "always be there." Perhaps we forget that friendships need to be kept current, that letting them languish is a sign of disrespect. Perhaps we don't know that maintaining a close bond with our women friends not only makes us feel better, but it just might save our lives.

"CHERYL, YOU'VE BEEN SEEING YOUR FAMILY AGAIN, HAVEN'T YOU?"

THIS IS NOT THE LIFE I ORDERED

Tending and Befriending

According to a landmark study conducted at UCLA, our connections to women friends actually counteract the stress most of us experience on a daily basis. Engaging in "tending and befriending" produces a calming effect. Our women friends soothe us, give us encouragement, and help us remember who we really are. We need to make time for nurturing these relationships and facilitating these conversations.

A famed Nurses' Health Study from Harvard Medical School found that the more women friends you have, the less likely you are to develop physical impairments as you age and the more likely you are to lead a joyful and meaningful life. In fact, the results were so significant that the researchers concluded that not having close friends or confidants was as detrimental to a woman's health as smoking or carrying extra weight. Don't let one more minute pass without reaching out to a woman friend. Build a way to connect with another woman into your daily routine.

13
DON'T BELIEVE THAT TO SUCCEED YOU MUST BE "MORE LIKE A MAN."

For women there are undoubtedly great difficulties in the path but so much more to overcome. Being a woman is not one of them. First, no woman should say, "I am but a woman." What more can you dare ask for or dare to be?

MARIA MITCHELL, ASTRONOMER AND FIRST WOMAN MEMBER OF THE AMERICAN ACADEMY OF ARTS AND SCIENCES HALL OF FAME (1818–1889)

Think Like a Woman

Deborah traded a college campus for corporate life, where she quickly learned that success came packaged in male clothing and testosterone-driven mind-sets. "It should never have happened to me," she claims. "Very strong and highly intelligent women mentored me. I worked for the Dean of Women at my university as a student when she was among the most powerful women in the country. I had also been a student of two pioneering researchers, Eleanor Maccoby and Carol Jacklin, who wrote the landmark book *The Psychology of Sex Differences*. At twenty-three, I couldn't have been more prepared, more ready to take my place in corporate America with confidence, knowledge, and support. I was ready to blaze a trail."

In a matter of months, however, she had lost her ability to think like a woman. "I quickly learned what would be rewarded and what would not," she recalls. "I didn't fit in, so I embarked upon a course that would 'fix me.' I kept a copy of *Games Mother Never Taught You* in my desk, rereading chapters and thinking that, if I only tried, I could become more like the people around me. I took classes and training to overcome what I thought were my inabilities."

She began to dress differently; she reports, eschewing bright colors for button-down Oxford shirts and well-tailored suits. She cut her long hair short and even took a golf lesson, because all of the men seemed to play golf. She learned to play poker and read the sports page along with the *Wall Street Journal*, just so she could take part in office conversations. She quit wearing makeup, except for mascara—somehow she just couldn't part with mascara!

"Returning from a business trip that had taken me to fifteen different cities in seven days," she recalls, "I found a note from my boss asking me to justify my airfare expense along with a question that was meant to be a joke: 'While in New York, did you get your shopping fix?' That did it. I marched into my manager's office and told him that the entire company was made up of sexist men. I left his office, locked myself in a bathroom stall, and cried. After wiping the tears from my eyes and fixing the running mascara, I returned to my office, determined that no one would know my agony.

"PARTNER WANNABE, PASSED OVER AGAIN, LACKING GOLF GAME AND THE BALLS."

HAIKU LOWDOWN

"The next day, I was summoned to go to lunch with the president of our division, Wayne Oler. I was certain I was going to be fired. He placed me squarely in the hot seat and grilled me on why I thought the corporate culture was sexist. 'Why do you think it is so difficult for you to succeed? Why do you feel uncomfortable?'"

Well, since she thought she was going to be fired anyway, she decided to tell him the truth. Much to her shock, he concluded the lunch by saying that he agreed with her. Deborah was amazed. "He told me he wanted my help on changing the organizational culture, as he viewed it as detrimental to long-term success. He said he wanted talent, and he didn't care what gender his employees were as long as they were human! I am indebted to Wayne, as he was mentoring women leaders decades before it was fashionable to do so.

"Today, I wear makeup and do not own one Oxford button-down shirt. Heck, I even wear perfume! I make no apologies and I bring all of my talents to the table, not hiding them just because they are feminine. Now steeped in organizational systems, which I've studied for twenty years, I clearly see what was impossible for me to understand at twenty-three. Cultures have strong and homogenizing effects upon the people in the organization. Male-dominated cultures, over time, can make even the most competent and strong women begin to doubt themselves. The trick is never to be afraid to think like a woman.

"The skills and insights that women bring to organizations don't need to be changed or rearranged simply because they are feminine," says Deborah. "They need to be embraced and celebrated by corporations and cultures. Instead of trying to fix our feminine selves to fit the male standard, perhaps we need to continue to change the world of work to allow, accept, and even seek the different ways we women communicate and lead. Surprisingly, in the organizations that are enlightened enough to recognize the value of this, something miraculous happens. Men grow too!"

14
MOVE ON, MOVE UP,
OR MOVE OUT.

You can do one of two things: Just shut up, which is
something I don't find easy, or learn an awful lot very fast
and stand up for yourself!

JANE FONDA, ACTRESS (1937–)

Learn to Be Comfortable with Being Uncomfortable

In the age of Facebook and Instagram, we may think that everyone has a perfect and happy life. We may question: Why me? Why can't I have a life that isn't turned upside down by death, divorce, career-ending events, or a host of other madness and mayhem? Unfortunately, reality has a way of getting in the way. The "reality slap," as described by author and psychotherapist Russ Harris, knocks us down, takes away our normalcy, and challenges us on all fronts. Dr. Harris describes these times as a "reality gap"—on one side is the happy reality we want; on the other is what we have. "The bigger the gap," he warns, "the more painful the feelings that arise."

In our lives, we've experienced a collective container of more reality slaps and gaps than we'd hoped for. We've learned that discomfort and uncertainty travel together. It's paradoxical, but the more we can ride the waves of being uncomfortable and uncertain, the stronger we become and the faster we will rise. Aversion to uncomfortable times in our lives and the conflicts that often accompany them is a natural human tendency. Yet the fact is that, if you plan to live a life that matters and make a mark of distinction, you need to get really comfortable with being uncomfortable. It begins with taking inventory of the issues in our lives that need to be resolved or confronted in order to move on, move up, or move out.

Avoiding issues that come with bad times only weakens us. Facing those issues head-on, we become stronger and more in control of our lives. This often requires confrontation, but many of us fear confrontation because of the unfair labels women seem to end up carrying: "She's a bitch." "She's a real ball-buster." "She's the ice queen." "She's the iron lady." "She's unstable." "She's crazy." These are all common labels for women who confront issues in their lives. It may be that men are able to use confrontation more effectively because they don't get stuck with these labels. But is that fair?

Confrontation doesn't have to take place in loud, uncaring, and hostile ways. Yet we do believe that every woman should develop a set of tools for confronting people. We also need to be comfortable being on the receiving end of confrontation. Conflict resolution needs to be a part of our DNA. We need to accept that disagreements are part of life and are to be expected in any kind of relationship—from a marriage to a corporate merger, with children and colleagues, even with insurance companies! If we run from disagreement, if we pretend it doesn't exist or hide from it, we only hurt ourselves.

Have you ever seen a woman successfully stand up for herself and skillfully handle a disagreement? What did she do? Why did you admire the way she resolved the issues? How can you emulate her? Can you approach her and ask for her best-practice tips on dealing with difficult people or difficult situations?

Is there an issue right now you need to confront or negotiate? Try role-playing that situation with your kitchen-table group so you can practice your responses and develop your ability to think on your feet when dealing with aggression.

15
TRUST IN GOD, BUT ROW AWAY FROM ROCKS.

An expert is a person who has made all of the mistakes that can be made in a very narrow field.

NIELS BOHR, DANISH PHYSICIST (1885–1962)

They'll Take Care of Me

There is truth in the old adage: Trust in God, but row away from the rocks. We can't afford to be naïve. As women, we need to keep our eye on our own welfare and not depend on corporations or spouses to take care of us. Too many of us still believe that a handsome prince is going to ride in on a white horse and take care of us just like in the fairy tales. In today's world, however, the prince takes off in search of himself and the horse runs off with another woman, leaving us alone to fend for ourselves.

As Gerry Laybourne, co-founder of the Oxygen Network and Oprah Winfrey's former business partner, told us: "It's your life, and you have to be responsible for all of it. It's not your husband's or lover's or partner's or best friend's or company's life. You have to own it and live it."

THIS IS NOT THE LIFE I ORDERED

Jan Yanehiro trusted that the television station she had worked for (and made millions of dollars for) would take care of her after the show she had created was canceled. After all, she had racked up an impressive set of ratings and three Emmys over a fifteen-year run with the beloved daily television program she had created that came into the homes and hearts of millions of Americans.

In a matter of days, however, her contract with the network dropped from $200,000 per year to $26,000. Jan learned quickly that all who promised they would "take care of her" disappeared when the cold, hard facts of the new contract were spelled out. "I was devastated," she says. "I trusted that this company, where I had spent most of my adult life, would somehow take care of me. It was a big mistake," says Jan.

Nancy Pedot, former CEO of a major retail conglomerate, had a similar experience. Nancy was instrumental in taking her company from start-up to initial public offering in four short years. She appeared on the cover of *Business Week* and was a darling of Wall Street. In fact, Nancy was a rare breed: a female CEO of a publicly traded company—at the time, one of only three in the nation.

Nancy decided that her next goal was to spend more time with her teenage son. He would soon be on his way to college, and Nancy did not want to miss his remaining years at home. She submitted her resignation to the board of directors, trusting that those in charge would tell the truth about why she was leaving.

Without her permission or knowledge, the news of Nancy's departure was released in a manner that suggested she had been fired. Although Nancy was not sure of the rationale behind the decision, it did protect the stock from dropping, because, of course, Wall Street would never believe that a woman would leave a CEO position in order to spend more time with her family.

Nancy awoke to a barrage of television commentary and newspaper articles with stories of her dismissal. Imagine her surprise! Friends, former colleagues, and executives phoned

Nancy and spoke as if tragedy had struck. When she attempted to tell the truth—that she had chosen to step down and had not been fired—only her closest friends believed her. Nancy had trusted that things would be handled in a respectful and ethical way. But the media told a different story altogether.

Never Make Assumptions

Margaret Loesch is a five-time Emmy winner who built the Fox Kids Network from a start-up to the number-one children's television service in the country. Prior to her tenure at Fox, she had been president and CEO of Marvel Productions and Hanna-Barbera Productions, where she supervised the development of more than thirty television series. Michealene came to know Margaret through her former boss. "I always respected and admired who she was," she notes. "The one thing about Margaret that always stood out was her integrity."

When asked about this, Margaret said: "I've always tried to do the right thing. The truer you are to yourself, the less conflicted you will be in life. In my experience, many women are loyal and competent and often optimistic. While most people appreciate integrity and honesty, however, it's not necessarily what is rewarded in business, so we have to be brave and we have to take care of each other and ourselves.

"Every major mistake in my life has come from my making an assumption," Margaret claims. "The most career-impacting assumption I've made has been to believe that I would be taken care of. Never make assumptions. Today when I speak to women, I pass on this hard-learned wisdom: Don't assume someone will be there to take care of your interests. If they are there for you, that's a wonderful gift. But if not, you must be prepared. You must be responsible for yourself."

Moving On

Do you see yourself in Jan's or Nancy's or Margaret's stories? If so, simply consider it a naïve mistake, learn the lesson, and move on, as both Jan and Nancy have. There is no value in wallowing in what was done to you, no matter how unfair or undeserved it may have been. Resolve right now that you will move on.

Please know that many smart women have succumbed to the mistaken notion that they would be "taken care of." Take a few minutes to think through these questions before you answer them in your WIT Kit journal:

- Who do you believe is responsible for you?

- Do you own every aspect of your life?

- What nitty-gritty details have you left in the hands of others?

Then, write three things you will do to become more self-sufficient and less dependent on others.

16
LISTEN TO YOUR INNER VOICE.

Intuition is a natural consequence of self-esteem, the greatest power you can have. With it, you broaden your life into an adventure, because you know in your gut that you can handle the unknown.

CAROLINE MYSS, MEDICAL INTUITIVE AND WRITER (1952–)

Nagging Doubts

Ignoring intuition, that tiny voice inside, is a mistake every woman we know has made. Here we are, equipped with one of the most powerful tools on the planet, and we don't listen to it—until the intuitive voice reaches a crescendo of nagging doubts that we can no longer ignore.

Jackie has learned to trust that female voice inside. In her first run for legislative office, she was not supported by those in power. As a result, she had to take out a loan against her townhouse to pay for a television commercial that was needed. "I remember walking down the street with a copy of the signed promissory note in my hand," she recalls, "and realizing the implications if I lost the election. Yet, this tiny voice inside me kept me strong. I knew that I had done the right thing. In an election where thousands of votes were cast, I won by a mere 400 votes!"

"I think I realized the value of female intuition," says Deborah, "when one of the most successful businessmen in America told me that he made all of his big decisions with his intuition—a skill he had worked for years to develop. I realized I was neglecting to use a part of my natural talent that could serve me in a multitude of ways."

Your intuition can give you a competitive advantage in business and in life. It can serve as a warning system when you're at risk. It can also help you decide what to do when the flow of your life turns into a tsunami. From now on, keep your antennae attuned to that small voice within. When it speaks, listen and act accordingly. You won't regret following your intuition; you will only regret ignoring it.

17
REALIZE THAT RISKS ARE
PART OF THE PACKAGE.

If you have made serious mistakes, there is always another chance for you. What we call failure is not the falling down, but the staying down.

MARY PICKFORD, CANADIAN-BORN ACTRESS (1892–1979)

Take Wise Risks

Eunice Azzanni was a legendary partner at the international search firm Korn Ferry. She placed more women in leadership positions than anyone we know. Eunice had a wonderful mantra: *If you are not living on the edge, you are simply taking up too much room.* She reminds us that, in order to create the wonderful life every woman deserves, we simply cannot allow the arrows-in-the-back downside of being pioneers to stop us from forging ahead and taking risks. Jackie has likewise routinely advised women to "take the risk." Risk is always going to be a part of pursuing lives that fulfill us. And wise risks are always worth taking.

Do You Dare?

Looking at the CV of Gail Sheehy, you might think that she's glided right through life with no problems. Author of the iconic book *Passages,* she was also a founding writer of *New York Magazine*, a best-selling *New York Times* author, and a political writer for *Vanity Fair*. In fact, however, her career almost ended before it began.

"Married at twenty-three, a mother at twenty-four, and blindsided by divorce at twenty-eight," she tells us, "I found myself struggling, like many young women I meet today, to strike a balance between my personal life and my career. I had to scramble to pay the rent by working full-time. But to be present for my toddler, I had to give up my dream job. Could I really afford, as a woman in the sixties, to pursue a career as a freelance writer? Would anyone take me seriously? I could easily have given up—gotten a job selling Tupperware. But I didn't.

"We really only have two choices: play it safe, or take a chance. For me, pulling back because of fear has always made me feel worse. When I tried overcoming my fears by taking a leap—even if I didn't land on my feet the first time—it made me stronger. I developed an impulse to turn anxiety into action. When I fear," Gail declares, "I dare."

What is your attitude toward taking risks? Think back to a time when you really stretched yourself and went after something. Did you start your own business even though there was a chance of financial failure? Did you try an adventure sport like mountain climbing or skydiving? Did you go to a convention where you didn't know anyone? Did you dare to share an unpopular opinion at a staff meeting?

What was the outcome of that risk? Did it work out as you hoped? What was your process for deciding whether that risk was wise or rash? Did you find that, even if the risk didn't turn out perfectly, it was still worth it?

Write in your WIT Kit journal about a risk you're glad you took. Explain how it impacted you. Now, think of a risk you're considering. List all the possible consequences, good and bad. How could you benefit from taking this risk? How could you "lose"?

Make this risk you're contemplating the topic of your time during your next kitchen-table meeting. Get other members' opinions and check their input against your gut. If, after thinking this through, it seems as if it's a wise risk, go for it.

WIT KIT TOOLS FOR LEARNING TO LOVE MISTAKES

1. How can you develop a scientific mind-set toward mistakes, to see them as stepping-stones to success rather than as things to avoid or be ashamed of? Think about this question and then write your answer in your WIT Kit journal.

2. Make a list of three of your "best mistakes" in your WIT Kit journal. What are three things that went wrong, that you regretted doing or not doing, or that didn't turn out the way you wanted them to? What did you learn from those mistakes?

3. Finish this sentence: "From now on, when I make a mistake, I'm going to _____."

4. Make the topic of your next kitchen-table group The Best Mistakes We've Made. Acknowledge your top three mistakes in life and describe what you learned from each one. Be sure to have your WIT Kit journal with you so you can record important insights.

CHAPTER THREE

MAKE COURAGE AN EVERYDAY COMPANION

*You become courageous by
doing courageous acts . . .
Courage is a habit.*

**MARY DALY, AMERICAN
ACADEMIC AND THEOLOGIAN
(1928–2010)**

18

KNOW IT'S THE OBSTACLES IN THE STREAM THAT MAKE IT SING.

I want to know if you can get up after the night of grief and despair, weary and bruised to the bone, and do what needs to be done to feed the children.

ORIAH MOUNTAIN DREAMER, WRITER (1954–)

Courage Needs a Partner

Courage is essential to a survive-and-thrive lifestyle. Without it, we become wearied and beaten by life's inevitable challenges. Just as obstacles are needed in order for a stream to sing, courage always requires a crisis or a seemingly insurmountable problem to bring it to light. Many see the exercise of courage as a solitary journey. But we believe the journey is best walked with women friends who, literally and figuratively, "en-courage" us.

Women showing courage today seem to be everywhere—whether taking to the streets in the Women's March or bravely speaking out on sexual harassment in the MeToo movement. Even very young women, mere teenagers, inspire us with their courage as they stand up to lead a nation on gun violence. Throughout history, courageous women have always changed the world for the better.

The word "courage" stems from the French word *coeur*, which means "heart." Leave it to the French to uncover the secret that deep within our hearts we will find the will-power and tenacity to face and embrace life's hardships. The esteemed psychologist Rollo May said: "Just as one's heart helps our body to function, pumping blood to our physical organs, courage makes possible all the virtues of human kind. Without courage, we have no real and authentic life."

One of the beautiful aspects of courage is that it's conta-gious. The more you choose to act in spite of your fear, the easier it is to do so. In the pages that follow, we share the stories of some very brave women in hopes that their courage will prove contagious.

"MY WORLD'S COLLAPSING, YET SOMEHOW I MUSTER THE WILL TO EAT CHOCOLATE."

19
REALIZE THAT COURAGE OFTEN MEANS LETTING GO.

Nothing in life is to be feared. It is only to be understood.

MADAME MARIE CURIE, POLISH-BORN CHEMIST (1867–1934)

Holding On and Letting Go

Michealene had a gifted acting coach who instructed his students while in class to close their eyes and say something aloud. Whatever they said would become the mantra for the class that day. "It is so hard to let go," Michealene blurted out. Much to her embarrassment, the coach stopped the class, asked the students to open their eyes and, while looking directly at her, he said: "It is not hard to let go. It is more difficult to hold on. Imagine the cat holding on to the limb of a tree. The longer it holds on, the heavier its body becomes. What is hard is continuing to have the strength to hold on." "Backward, I had it all backward," Michealene realized. "Holding on to everything at all costs was what I had defined as strength. But letting go was the truly courageous act."

Letting go played a role in Sukey Forbes Bigham's act of courage. Sukey lived a charmed life, with a successful husband, a prominent career in the biotechnology field, and three beautiful children—Cabot, age eight; Charlotte, age six; and Beatrice, age three. Charlotte suffered from high fevers, but other than giving her parents some sleepless nights, it was not of serious concern. Yet over the summer, Sukey noticed that Charlotte was becoming very muscular, like a gymnast, for no apparent reason. Her sister-in-law, a nurse, suspected that Charlotte suffered from malignant hyperthermia, a condition in which the body is unable to cool itself down.

One August day when Charlotte wasn't feeling well, Sukey, on instinct, took her to the local hospital. By the time they arrived, Charlotte's fever had reached 102. The doctor was hesitant to admit Charlotte—fevers of 102 were common—but Sukey demanded that they do so and expressed her fear of malignant hyperthermia. Charlotte's fever continued to climb and, when it hit 108 degrees, she went into cardiac arrest. The doctors could not revive her and the beautiful six-year-old, who hours before had been full of life, was pronounced dead.

Sukey's charmed life was shattered. She described it to us like this: "When one suffers a great loss, the option pool for the next step is pretty grim. I saw three choices: choose to die, choose to exist until I die, or choose to live. The last option was the most difficult, but frankly it was the only

THIS IS NOT THE LIFE I ORDERED

option available. There is always a choice. I want women to remember that there is always a choice, and it resides within us to choose."

Positive Attitudes Are Underrated

"Losing Charlotte has been the most devastating experience of my forty years. I expect it to be the most devastating experience of my next forty. Since I can't wish my little girl back to life, I want to pull some lessons from her short life. When I see her again, I want to be able to tell her how profoundly her loss affected me—not in the negative and obvious ways, but in the ways that have made me a better person; in the ways that I hope to help other people; in the ways that I hope I am able to bring some of her gentle, impish spirit into all that I do while I remain here."

Sukey describes grief as a delicate dance. "It is two steps forward, two steps back, and then sometimes a huge dip. The process of letting go is healing, yet it requires something difficult when love is involved. It is easy to be utterly immersed in the pain of loss. That fullness keeps the loss very present. The hard part is letting go of some of the weight and still feeling connected. I have not mastered that. All I know is that the next forty-plus years, the time I need to wait until I see my daughter again, will go by much more quickly if I can somehow find a way to get back into life. To find joy. To stay vital and to stay in love with possibilities.

"Positive attitudes are underrated," Sukey claims. "Without one, I would still be in bed right now. Some days it comes easier than others, but I am determined. I owe that to my surviving children, to my husband, to Charlotte, to myself. The hardest part in the process was 'letting go' of the grief so I could be fully available to help my children and my husband get through their own grief."

Are you in the middle of a heart-breaking situation where the real act of courage is to let go of grief, resentment, or anger? What is that situation? What are the consequences of hanging on? What are the benefits of letting go?

20
DEVELOP A FUNNY BONE.

It is better to be a lion for a day than a sheep all of your life.

ELIZABETH KENNY, AUSTRALIAN NURSE (1880–1952)

Stressed Is Desserts Spelled Backward

In February 1999, Saranne Rothberg heard those dreaded words—malignant tumor, breast cancer, surgery, radiation, chemo—and she felt as if she had forgotten how to breathe.

"The medical staff continued to banter about the prognosis for my exposed breasts when suddenly my mind rebelled," she relates. "I'd read a magazine article about Norman Cousins, who had 'laughed himself well.' In the middle of my diagnosis, that article hijacked my thoughts. The diagnosing doctor had just informed me it was too late on a Friday to assemble their hospital cancer squad. With that, and with what I readily admit might have been a slightly hysterical reaction, I yanked off my hospital gown and ran from the medical center to the local video store in search of comedy tapes."

THELMA TAKES HER ANXIETIES TO THE STREETS.

In the video store, Saranne was like an emotional Grand Canyon of fear, anxiety, and depression. If laughing had helped Norman Cousins heal his rare nerve disease two decades ago, she wondered, why couldn't she amuse her cancer for sixty hours? What did she have to lose? Armed with stacks of stand-up comedy performances and feature films, she returned home still reeling from the logistics of what it meant to fight cancer. She wooed her five-year-old daughter to bed earlier than usual and started coming to terms with her diagnosis.

"I was barely holding back a flood of tears as we said her prayers," Saranne remembers. "Torturous questions bombarded my mind: How many more bedtime stories will I read to her? Will I be strong enough to bathe her after chemo starts? Sobbing, I ran to the television in the other room and fumbled to insert the first videotape. Could the comedy cavalry rescue me the way Norman Cousins had documented in his article?"

Saranne sat in front of the monitor, praying for a miracle. A young Eddie Murphy appeared on the screen, set up his first joke, delivered the punch line, and the audience's laughter filled the room. "I demanded that my mind listen to Eddie even though it was more interested in self-chatter about my own mortality," she admits. "Then another Murphy joke; I laughed and blew my nose. Another joke; I laughed and cried. Another joke; more guffaws from deep inside. I could still laugh! I realized the cancer that was ravaging my healthy breast tissue couldn't rob me of my ability to laugh unless I let it." She switched to a Jackie Mason video and with each laugh came a deeper breath. With each deeper breath came relaxation. With relaxation came a sense of welcomed calm. She was now laughing multiple times per minute, and life seemed manageable again.

"As the East Coast went to sleep, Robin Williams' genius caused me to laugh without pause. His manic antics jiggled all those stomach knots caused by the cancer diagnosis. Next, my cancerous left breast and I started laughing at Jerry

Seinfeld's 'Lost Socks in the Dryer' monologue. I slapped my knees in shared mirth—I lose half a pair every time I do laundry.

"Then, it hit me. I am not alone. Millions of people are going through this cancer journey too. We're supposed to connect. Like everyone else diagnosed with a life-threatening illness, I was stressed. But with the help of Norman Cousins and myriad other comics, I received a crash course in comic perspective. Their humorous outlook on life instilled in me the determination to continue to laugh even while undergoing my dark nights of the soul.

"It's been almost five years, three surgeries, forty-four radiation treatments, and too many chemo cocktails since my all-night comedy marathon. I am now considered cancer-free," Saranne relates. And at least twice a day, she connects with comedy as a tribute to Norman Cousins and all the comics who have given her a new life's mission at the Comedy Cures Foundation. "From its grassroots launch during my first chemo treatment," she claims, "it became clear that I had been given a unique opportunity to bring joy and humor to others through this nonprofit service. And the punch line? My funny bone, once fractured, is now healed."

You can visit *www.comedycures.com* to learn more about what Saranne and her sidekicks at Comedy Cures are up to.

How do you keep your sense of humor when things aren't going your way? Fun is not frivolous. Keeping your "wit" about you is vital to maintaining a positive perspective in the midst of negative events.

Why not post your favorite cartoons and funny quotes where you can see them all the time? It's a way to feed your funny bone on a daily basis, to lighten up instead of tighten up. And remember: Stressed is desserts spelled backward.

21
WALK THROUGH FIELDS OF FEAR

Not truth, but faith, it is that keeps the world alive.

EDNA ST. VINCENT MILLAY, POET (1892–1950)

The Killing Fields

Letting go of fear opens up space for courage to come into our lives. Yet fear can be one of the most difficult obstacles to overcome as a woman struggles to rise to the surface in a life that keeps dragging her down. Whenever we become fearful, we think of Vornida Seng. She says that someday she will tell her children what happened to her. And the story she will tell begins when Khmer Rouge soldiers burst into her home.

Vietnamese dictator Pol Pot had decided that, in order to create the perfect communist state, he would first empty the cities of Cambodia. "Thousands of people filled the streets," Vornida recalls. "Corpses lay by the road. Hospital patients, some with IV bottles, tried to walk with the crowd. I began to walk, and I walked for weeks. We reached a village near the Thailand border. I was eleven at the time and, along with my mother and siblings, was forced to work twelve hours a day in the rice fields."

Vornida's family built their own primitive hut from the surrounding bamboo trees. Her grandmother and sister contracted malaria and, within days, her grandmother was dead. Three weeks later, Vornida's little sister, her eyes open and full of tears, died in her lap. Her mother, starving like most of the villagers, died and left her to care for her remaining siblings—her brother Siphano, nine, her brother Visothy, eight, and her sister Methegany, ten. They were sent to a mountain prison camp, where Visothy died in Vornida's arms of high fever and starvation. Soldiers tied little Siphano to a tree. Vornida describes the scene: "His eyes were shut, and the soldiers kept hitting him with their rifles. They brought bees and ants to sting him until he lost consciousness." He died shortly thereafter.

In 1978, the Pol Pot regime started to crumble. Carrying her remaining sister, Methegany, in a basket, Vornida started to walk again. She walked hundreds of miles to a neighboring village and hitched a ride to the province of Siem Reap in a frantic search for a hospital. A few days later, Methegany died.

With the death of the last of her siblings, Vornida believed her life and dreams were over. Then, a local driver for *Time* magazine took her in and alerted the Bangkok bureau chief. *Time* sponsored Vornida, paid her passage to the United States, and gave her the job she continues to hold today in New York City. Vornida Seng believes that God meant for her to survive for a reason. When she looks into the eyes of her two small children, she says: "My family lives on in them."

Learn to Walk Through Fear

The next time you feel fear creeping into your life, remember the inspirational story of Vornida Seng. Fear did not stop Vornida as she made her way across her native country. Fear did not prevent her from building a new life, from finding love, or from starting a family again in her new world. Vornida could easily have chosen to live the rest of her life in denial or depression. Who could have blamed her? Yet she did not. She kept walking through life, putting one foot in front of the other. She chose to believe that the suffering she and her family had experienced could serve some higher purpose.

Have you been devastated by a tragedy? Are you mourning the loss of a loved one? Has something happened to you or someone close to you that is deeply unfair? Are you fearful of the future?

Putting one foot in front of the other—taking one step at a time, one day at a time—will bring you closer to the life you want. When Vornida was working in the rice fields, starving in a mountain prison camp, and fleeing her country on foot, she had no way of knowing that she would one day be gifted with two healthy children, a satisfying job, and her own home. Vornida is proof of the tenacity of the human spirit and its ability to transcend fears and tragic circumstances. She is a living, breathing testimony to what we can do if we choose to persevere through pain and walk through fear.

22
BE BRAVE ON YOUR OWN BEHALF.

When you get to the end of your rope, tie a knot in it and hang on.

**ELEANOR ROOSEVELT, FORMER
FIRST LADY (1884–1962)**

The Mom from Petaluma

Denise Garibaldi was a soft-spoken and heart-broken woman from a small town when we first met. The mom from Petaluma, California, touched the nation with her poignant testimony to Congress in what became a historic congressional hearing on anabolic steroids and their increasing use by high school, college, and professional athletes. Sitting directly behind such baseball legends as Sammy Sosa and Jose Canseco during the House Government Reform Committee hearings, Denise witnessed one major league baseball player after another refuse to discuss, or outright deny, allegations that they had used steroids.

Why was Denise at the hearing? Three years earlier, her son Rob had committed suicide as a result of a deep depression brought on by his steroid use. As a senior in high school, he had been a gifted baseball player; the New York Yankees had drafted him, but he had chosen instead to accept a scholarship to play for the University of Southern California.

Spurred on by coaches and trainers who told him he needed to "get bigger in order to become better," Rob turned to anabolic steroids. He defended his actions by telling his parents that this was what all professional baseball players did. He said: "Mom, these are not drugs. They're supplements, and all the major-league players use them." He backed up his claim by naming several well-known athletes who had admitted in TV interviews they used these "harmless" supplements. Denise struggled to save her son, placing him in rehabilitation clinics and arranging for private therapy. Unfortunately, she could not wrestle him away from the drug's powerful grip and its damaging effects.

After Rob's death, Denise began to speak out about the trainers and coaches who she believed contributed to her son's death. Many tried to intimidate her into silence, threatening her with lawsuits. But her courage grew threefold, and she joined forces with other parents who were coming forward to tell their own heartbreaking stories.

A Mom on a Mission

In less than a year, we witnessed Denise become a "mom on a mission" as she garnered a worldwide audience for her important message. Denise, who otherwise would never have sought a national spotlight, told us the day before her congressional testimony that she derived her courage from her hope that Rob's life and death would not be forgotten. Her goal was to alert parents to the dangers of steroids and to save them and their families from the pain and loss she had experienced.

She said: "It is also my time to tell our national heroes, the ones our children look up to, that players who take steroids and other performance-enhancing drugs are not only cheaters, but cowards. I want them to stand up and be counted. I want them to show our children a different way to compete at the top levels so we can put an end to this madness. They hide behind their unions with the help of management and powerfully connected people. Too many famous athletes and sports teams have resisted facing this issue. How many more Robs are out there trying to emulate their heroes, not knowing this path can lead to an early death?"

Rock the Boat

Is there something going on around you that is not right? Are you afraid to voice your concerns because you were taught not to rock the boat? Do you consider yourself shy, timid, or soft-spoken? That didn't stop Denise. We're not suggesting you be rash, but we are suggesting that silence changes nothing. If you feel strongly that something you're witnessing is wrong, then you have a responsibility to bring it to the attention of whoever is in a position to do something about it. All of us have had to confront an individual or organization that "wronged" us. It wasn't easy. Yet we all are glad we didn't suffer in silence and allow the inappropriate situation to continue.

23
EARN YOUR OWN RED BADGE OF COURAGE.

Character contributes to beauty. It fortifies a woman. Her mode of conduct, a standard of courage, discipline, fortitude, and integrity, can do a great deal to make a woman beautiful.

JACQUELINE BISSET, MODEL AND ACTRESS (1944–)

The Steely Look of Resolve

We had bumper stickers created for one of Jackie's political campaigns that read: The Courage to Lead. That slogan served to remind us on a daily basis of the inspiration we'd received from knowing Jackie. If there really were a red badge of courage, we would award it to Jackie Speier.

"I was with Jackie in the hospital the day she had to decide to take her husband off life support," says Deborah. "Three months pregnant at the time, and in the midst of devastating grief, Jackie focused on the best way to break the news to Jackson, her five-year-old son. After the funeral, I sat next to her on the sofa in her living room. Newly widowed, she was also six weeks away from impending bankruptcy. The pain of that day was overwhelming, yet Jackie remained focused on the options available to her. She endured."

Deborah tells of another time when she sat next to Jackie at an awards dinner. She was the only one in the audience who knew that Jackie was wearing a bulletproof vest due to threats against her life resulting from her attempts to pass legislation that would sanction the wages of absent fathers who were in arrears on child-support payments. "In the restroom, before the dinner began," Deborah reports, "Jackie pulled open her blouse to show me the bulletproof vest. We both agreed that it added extra inches to her cleavage, but that it was a heck of a way to achieve a better figure!"

Several years later, Jackie faced down the financial and banking industries in a high-stakes endeavor to pass a privacy bill that protected Californians' personal and financial information. Astoundingly, nearly $20 million in special-interest funds rolled into the pockets of lawyers, lobbying groups, and industry veterans, all aimed directly at derailing Jackie Speier. During the evening news that night, Deborah saw Jackie on television and noticed the look in her eyes. "I knew at that precise moment that $20 million and a well-connected contingent of bankers, lawyers, and lobbyists were no match for my friend Jackie."

Courage in Everyday Life

The steely look of resolve in Jackie's eyes resurfaced after she decided to speak out on corruption and inefficiencies in the California state prison system. The powerful California Correctional Peace Officers Association (CCPOA), a union composed of prison guards, targeted her in a series of public-relations ploys. They organized a large rally at Raley Field in Sacramento, where more than 5,000 people gathered. From the podium, leaders of the CCPOA painted Jackie as their enemy. On the streets of Sacramento, these same people handed out phony dollar bills that carried derogatory statements about her. "Yet they could not see what I saw," Deborah reports.

"Behind the enormous desk in her Senate chambers, I viewed the silhouette of the woman I have known for most of my adult life. She looked so small. After all, she stands only five feet four inches tall and, even on a day when she and her staff have binged on chocolate, she only weighs in at about 120 pounds. Yet I knew the CCPOA had met their match in the petite, feminine, and unflinchingly strong Jackie Speier."

Several days later, Jackie told Deborah something she will always remember. She said: "Deborah, after my life experiences, I have nothing left to fear. Where I see wrong, I will do my best to make it right, no matter the cost. The worst thing that can happen is that I'll lose an election. That does not seem like a very big price to pay considering what I have already lived through."

Today Jackie continues to unleash that undaunting courage on a national stage. *Newsweek* magazine named her among the 150 most fearless women leaders in the world. After a decade of serving in the United States House of Representatives, Jackie has challenged the highest levels of leadership in the military and on college campuses on issues of sexual assault. As a member of the House Intelligence and Homeland Security Committees, she has doggedly pursued truth in investigating Russian interference in democracy. "When I am feeling intimidated, defeated, derailed, or depressed, I often think of Jackie," says Deborah. "Her example always motivates me to move forward instead of shrinking back and wilting."

Who is your shining example? Whom do you admire as a walking, talking role model of courage? Is it your mom? Mahatma Gandhi? Your sister? Your aunt? Eleanor Roosevelt? Or a woman business owner you respect? Is it a neighbor who participates in the March Against Breast Cancer each year?

What is it about these people that causes you to respect them? Can you think of a specific situation in which they held their heads high and forged ahead despite daunting circumstances? In your WIT Kit journal, describe what happened and the choices they made to face their fears rather than flee from them. What challenging situation are you facing? How would your role model handle it? Plan exactly what you are going to say and do so you can resolve that situation with courage.

24
LET YOURSELF CRY WHEN TINKER BELL DIES.

Love has pride in nothing—but its own humility.

CLARE BOOTH LUCE, CONGRESSWOMAN AND DIPLOMAT (1903–1987)

The Courage to Stay

Courage can appear as cowardice from the outside—until we look more closely. Take, for example, infidelity in marriage. Among us, three discovered unfaithful husbands. When we shared our heartbreak with one another, our opinions ranged from "Dump the jerk," to "Get a divorce," to "Can this marriage be saved?"

One of us remembers discovering her husband's affair. She says: "I felt alone and devastated by his infidelity. I felt like Tinker Bell, believing that the world was wonderful while living with a man like Peter Pan, whom I hoped would eventually grow up. I remember quite clearly the day I realized that I was living a 'make-believe' life. I was pregnant at the time, and I went to get an AIDS test because my husband had confessed to an affair and to having unprotected sex that put our child and me at risk. As I sat in the hallway of that tiny laboratory waiting for my test, I shared my secret with the nurse. Surprisingly, she told me that I was the third pregnant and married woman that week to come in for the same reason. Gee, I thought, maybe I should start a club!

THIS IS NOT THE LIFE I ORDERED

"HONEY, I'M RUNNING OUT FOR 30 OR 40 YEARS. THERE'S FOOD IN THE FRIDGE."

"I was pregnant, unhappy, and confused. One day, I was leaving. The next day, I was kicking him out of our home. My rampant hormones from the pregnancy, mixed with the emotions surrounding his betrayal, made me almost suicidal. I remembered other women—far too many—who had had to deal with their husbands' betrayals being covered as front-page news because they just happened to involve the leader of the free world, the governor of a state, or a member of the royal family. I recalled editorials and talk-show hosts constantly debating 'Should she stay or go?' The women who chose to stay were criticized incessantly for their decision. They were portrayed as weak or less than independent and strong women. I, on the other hand, knew that the choice they had made required an extreme act of courage—the courage to stay.

"It takes as much courage to stay in a relationship and face pain, anger, and betrayal as it does to leave. After I made the decision to stay, it took two years of heart-breaking and excruciating work to repair our marriage. Rebuilding trust with someone who has been unfaithful and learning to forgive that person sometimes seemed harder than getting a divorce would have been.

"Today, I have a strong relationship with my husband—better than at any previous point in our marriage. He is a conscious, loving father and an adult man, fully responsible for his actions and their effects upon others. He almost lost his family, but through the experience, we gained so much more. Although we've had a happy ending, the sadness over what happened didn't just disappear. Tinker Bell no longer lives in my heart. She left for Neverland. But in her place she left the mature, 'real-life' marriage that my husband and I now share.

Courage is about doing what's right for you. Make a conscious choice about your plan of action rather than bowing to pressure or pretending that everything is just fine. Are you in a relationship? How would you describe it? If it's everything you want it to be, congratulations. If the other person is not treating you with the love or respect you want or deserve, what are you going to do about it?

25
WEAR A COURAGE BRACELET.

I've been absolutely terrified every moment of my life—and I've never let it keep me from doing a single thing I wanted to do.

GEORGIA O'KEEFFE, ARTIST (1887–1986)

Sweaty Palms

Our friend, Gary Heil, wears a wristband given to him by a former NBA player. On the wristband are three words: Goals, Attitude, Courage. The words serve as a constant reminder for Gary to reflect on these questions:

- Am I clear about what I want to accomplish?

- Am I clear about who I am?

- Do I have the courage to be authentic even when it is tough?

- Do I have the courage to commit to the truth and do the right thing, not the expeditious thing?

- Am I positive and optimistic even in the face of failure?

The change that answering these questions made in Gary's interactions with others was remarkable, so Deborah decided to make her own bracelet. She bought a leather strap and seven crystal letter charms that spelled out the word "courage."

"Looking at the word 'courage' each day has had a powerful effect upon me," she reports. "It reminds me to be authentic in times of difficulty, to tell the truth even when it hurts, to be confident in my choices, and to remember that courage is within me waiting to be called upon. It may sound simplistic, but if I find myself in an uncomfortable situation, I just look at the word and it gives me strength I didn't feel a moment before."

Don't Sit in the Audience of Life

A wise woman once said: "Sitting in the audience can be easier than taking center stage. It takes a great deal of courage to go from being part of the crowd to being in front of the crowd." We owe it to ourselves and all those we care about to take center stage willingly and eagerly. We believe taking center stage was what Marianne Williamson meant when she said: "Our deepest fear is not that we are inadequate. Our deepest fear is that we are powerful beyond measure. It is our light, not our darkness that frightens us." We ask ourselves who we are that we should expect to be brilliant, gorgeous, talented, fabulous. Actually, the better question is who are you not to be. There's nothing enlightened about shrinking back so that other people won't feel insecure around you. Thinking small helps no one.

26
KNOW THAT COURAGE ISN'T ONLY FOR HEROES.

I don't want to be remembered as the girl who was shot. I want to be remembered as the girl who stood up.

MALALA YOUSAFZAI, NOBEL PRIZE WINNER (1997–)

Courage Roars When You Find Your Voice

Courage can save lives, tell truths, and help us face life-altering situations. Yet courage does not have to be played out on a national stage. As Mary Anne Radmacher, says: "Courage doesn't always roar. Sometimes courage is the quiet voice at the end of the day saying, 'I will try again tomorrow.'"

Philosopher Ruth Gordon said it best when she described courage as a muscle that is strengthened by its own use. We women need to give ourselves credit for the things we do each day that are courageous—deciding to propose an idea in a meeting, asking for a well-deserved raise, holding a colleague accountable for an unfulfilled commitment. Each time we face facts instead of running from them, we build our courage muscles.

Today, we are witnessing many women exercising their courage muscles as they tell the world that they will no longer stand for situations that are unfair, unjust, or biased. They are declaring that most "isms" must be banished— racism, sexism, ageism, to name but a few. Before the MeToo movement, we never talked publicly about sexual harassment, but carried around our own personal stories for many years. We were told, in whispered voices, that it was just the way of the world and we had to find strategies for dealing with the unfortunate experiences and bad behaviors.

Jan says it happened to her in her first job in radio. A powerful man made advances; she tried to ignore them but they continued unabated. Looking back now, she wonders why she tolerated it. At that time, she was young and new to her career; she had yet to find her voice.

Michealene had her fair share of harassment in the entertainment industry. Speaking out during that time was very career limiting, but she and other women in the industry warned young women which powerful men to avoid and which ones they should never be alone with.

Jackie recently told the nation in a very public forum that she too was a MeToo who had carried her secret around for years. She recalls that, as a twenty-three-year-old congressional staffer excited about her new job, her enthusiasm was dulled when the chief of staff got her alone in a room. The fifty-year-old man grabbed her face and stuck his tongue down her throat. Since she went public with her story, Jackie has also introduced legislation to stream-line harassment reporting procedures and to shed light on the big settlements paid out of taxpayers' money to silence harassment complaints.

Calling Foul

While it's becoming easier to stand up and speak out, these issues still require a great deal of courage to address—courage that Anucha Brown Sanders found many years ago. When we met Anucha, she was Vice President of Women's Basketball for the NCAA in Indianapolis. After Anita Hill and before the MeToo movement, Anucha stood alone on a national stage and filed a complaint against a famous and powerful man who had sexually harassed her at work.

At the time, Anucha was the highest-ranking female executive of her favorite childhood team, the New York Knicks. Her dream-come-true job turned into a national nightmare, however, when a powerful Knicks executive verbally abused and sexually harassed her repeatedly. Less than a month after filing a formal complaint against him, she was fired.

Anucha's court case spanned two years, during which she experienced a very public and ruthless assault upon her reputation, her competence, and even her sanity. Yet her courage did not waiver. The jury decided in her favor and ordered the Knicks to pay her $11.6 million in punitive damages. Many years later, Anucha says that she still receives letters from women who tell her that they found their own voice because of her actions. She told our audience: "I hope you will remember that no matter your situation, you do not ever have to put up with bad behavior. You do have the power to confront it." Courage roars when you find your voice.

Have you been discriminated against? Have you allowed people's prejudices to hold you back from achieving what you wanted or deserved? How can you "kick through" limitations placed on you by other people, cultures, or stereotypes?

In your WIT Kit journal, write about any situation in which you feel you have not fulfilled your potential. What's holding you back? Are the obstacles external or internal? Make this the topic of your kitchen-table group. Discuss this challenge and ask your friends for their advice on how you can climb the "mountains" on the path to your goals.

WIT KIT TOOLS FOR MAKING COURAGE AN EVERYDAY COMPANION

1. In your WIT Kit journal, draw a vertical line down the center of the page to divide it into two columns. Label the column on the left Imagined Fears and the column on the right Real Fears. Imagined fears are intellectual or emotional fears that exist only in your head or heart. Real fears are based on something tangible—something that can be seen, that poses an actual risk to your safety or the safety of your loved ones. Start listing everything you're afraid of in the appropriate columns. This can include anything from the fear of ending up alone to the fear that your preteen is having sex. They can be professional fears ("I'm not going to get that promotion I've been promised") or personal fears ("What's that suspicious-looking mole on my back?").

2. Revisit the lists and write down the worst thing that could happen and the best thing that could happen in each scenario. Ask yourself if the worst that can happen has been exaggerated in your mind. What are the odds of it happening? What can you do to prevent it from happening? What steps can you take to reverse or resolve that situation?

3. Now, focus on the best thing that could happen. How can you foster a positive outcome? Who can help you? What three specific steps can you take to start acting on that fear instead of avoiding it?

CHAPTER 4

UNDERSTANDING MONEY

*I'm not afraid of money at all.
Money is power. It will give me
power to do things truer to my
spirit than what I'm already doing.*

**TYRA BANKS,
PRODUCER, BUSINESS WOMAN,
ACTRESS, AUTHOR, AND MODEL
(1973–)**

27
WHEN YOU ARE SHORT ON DOLLARS, BE RICH IN SPIRIT.

I've been rich and I've been poor. Rich is better.

GRETA GARBO, SWEDISH ACTRESS (1905–1990)

Self-Made Women

We four are all "self-made" women, born into working-class families where living from paycheck to paycheck was the norm. Combined, we have more than 250 years of life experience. Collectively, during our lives, we have bought and sold thirty-two homes, purchased forty cars, and were the primary decision-makers on life insurance, health insurance, auto insurance, bank accounts, broker-age accounts, and disposable diapers. We've bought enough groceries to fix approximately 252,000 meals, and enough laundry detergent, hair spray, diet soda, bottled water, computers, and flat screen TVs to fill a large gymnasium. We've stayed in over 8,000 hotel rooms from New York to San Francisco, from London to Shanghai, and in Osh Kosh, Wisconsin.

We are the living, breathing demographic of the female consumer who decides over 80 percent of the consumer purchases made, 50 percent of all electronics bought, and 50 percent of all personal computers sold. Women are responsible for nine out of every ten checks written in the United States and nearly 82 percent of us are in charge of the family finances. We decide which baker feeds our families, which company provides our health care, which cell phone maker keeps us in touch, and what share of the family budget flows to which consumer brands. Yet, when it comes to finances, we have made some embarrassing mistakes. Our financial DNA has been placed on life-support several times.

We four carry a dirty, little secret that far too many women share. We believed that the men in our lives were smarter about money than we are. When that proved not to be true, we were left to pick up the pieces. We have lost homes, jobs, and businesses due to this misplaced belief. We have had to negotiate with the IRS on back taxes we didn't know our spouses owed (and didn't think we could be held accountable for). We've been involved in lawsuits in which we were implicated by virtue of our marriage licenses. We've lived as two-income families suddenly transformed into one-income families and, at several times due to lay-offs and re-structuring, to no-income families! In retrospect, we realized that our financial issues always seemed to coincide with our major life transitions. But that meant that our financial crises could either become a source of growth or remain a crippling burden. The outcome depended simply on how we chose to act.

Women Hold the Purse Strings

Women have come a long way financially, especially considering that it wasn't until 1974 that we could even get a credit card in our own names. Today, women hold 60 percent of all personal wealth in the United States and 51 percent of all stocks. Over a million of us make in excess of $100,000 per year and we run 40 percent of all private businesses. As a group, we earn more than $12 trillion every year. Breaking glass ceilings and becoming educated has truly improved our financial standing.

Yet, somewhere along the line, too many of us neglected to take responsibility for our financial health. In a world where women hold the purse strings, the following is still reality:

- Women are first in America's growing hunger class.

- We live near the brink of poverty, when you consider that the difference between a mother on welfare and most other mothers is nothing more than a partner's paycheck.

- We are unlikely to have a pension plan, yet we tend to live seven to nine years longer than the men in our lives.

- Fifty percent of us will become widows by the age of fifty-three, and 50 percent of us will divorce in our lifetimes.

- When we divorce, we are five times more likely to live in poverty after retirement than married women.

- For every year that we leave the workforce to care for a child or a parent, it will take us five years to make up the difference in our retirement and pension plans—if we have them.

- Amidst this changing landscape, women and families with children at home have become two of the fastest growing groups filing for personal bankruptcy—a staggering increase of almost 662 percent over the past decade.

Who are the women reflected in these numbers? They are all of us. What brings women to the brink of bankruptcy? It is not long-term problems involving chronic over-spending. Rather the most common reasons are sudden financial setbacks caused by job loss, illness or injury, medical debt, or divorce.

These facts are unacceptable. Yet they remain facts and, from the hundreds of interviews we've conducted, we believe that almost every woman will incur a serious financial setback in her lifetime. We can and must educate ourselves about money so we become smarter about the way we make it, manage it, and invest it. The ability to rise above financial ruin is within your grasp—if you learn from our mistakes and take action in some of the ways we're about to share with you.

28
LEARN THE LESSONS FROM THE DREAM HOUSE ON CHATEAU DRIVE.

There are no hopeless situations. There are only people who have grown hopeless about them.

**CLARE BOOTH LUCE, CONGRESSWOMAN
AND DIPLOMAT (1903–1987)**

In Just That Moment

Jackie remembers their home on Chateau Drive. It was primarily financed by the "three days on and three days off" shifts her husband worked as an emergency-room physician. Little did she know their dream house would soon belong to someone else. Someone who would never know about the Easter egg hunts elaborately planned and conducted in the backyard. Someone who would never transform the living room into a magical winter wonderland in December. To someone else, it would simply be a good investment. Yet to Jackie, the home was where her son had his own room, complete with a bright-red bunk bed his dad gave him on his fifth birthday. It was where her unborn child had been conceived.

"I remember so vividly our conversation regarding his life insurance," Jackie says. "I kept nagging him to renew it. He told me he was too busy to take the required physical exam. He got tired of me bringing it up and yelled: 'Jackie! Are you planning to have me done away with? Is that why you are so persistent about this?' I dropped the subject. Three months later, he was dead. I was left with an unborn child and a five-year-old son, and I had less than forty-five days to vacate our dream house on Chateau Drive—a house I could no longer afford."

Today, Jackie plays back that conversation about life insurance in her mind and wishes she could return to that moment in time. "I wish I had said: 'Steve, this situation is not about me. It is about our children and their quality of life if something happens to you. I am not being morbid. I am being financially responsible.'"

Since it's impossible for Jackie to have this conversation with Steve now, she has it with hundreds of women each year in the presentations she gives. "I beg women to stop being naïve," she declares. "I implore them to have this tough conversation with their spouses, even if they don't want to talk about it. I explain that what happened to me can and will happen to far too many women."

Are you on top of your financial situation? Are you and your spouse adequately covered by life and medical insurance? How much debt are you carrying? What type of savings or investments do you have to carry you over if you encounter tough times? If you can't answer these questions, you are tempting fate.

Promise yourself that you will sit down with your spouse or partner, and preferably with a knowledgeable and impartial third party like a financial planner or advisor whom you can trust. Discuss all aspects of your financial health and establish a plan so you can sleep at night knowing that you and your family will be provided for if your income disappears or drastically changes.

29
DON'T WAIT UNTIL YOUR FINANCIAL DNA IS ON LIFE SUPPORT.

Money is always there, but the pockets change. It is not in the same pocket after a change, and that is all there is to say about money.

GERTRUDE STEIN, WRITER (1874–1946)

Simply Because We Are Women

Why do women take frequent financial tumbles? We interviewed several respected financial experts to help us understand why. This complex issue became a little clearer when they told us that women, as a whole, still earn less money than men. The US Labor Department documents that women working full-time earn only 80 percent of what men earn. More than one-fourth of us head families with incomes of less than $20,000 per year. Ouch!

Some of this occurs simply because we are women. Women's work patterns tend to lead to lower earnings. Due to pregnancy, childcare, and caregiving, we spend an average of ten years away from work (versus one year for men). For every year we stay out of the workforce, it takes us five years to recover lost income, pension coverage, and career advancement. Over a lifetime, the inequality in our pay (80 cents on the dollar) costs a woman $300,000.

Another piece of the puzzle is that women tend to live longer than men, which means we face a higher risk of outliving our assets or suffering chronic or disabling diseases that cut into our earning potential. We also routinely drain our bank accounts to pay the healthcare costs of a seriously ill husband, sick child, or ailing parent. Women pay a huge financial penalty for being the primary caregivers in the United States. According to an AARP/Brandeis University study, the loss of earned income due to women leaving the workforce to provide care is a staggering $678,664 over a woman's lifetime.

Several investment counselors also told us that they believe many women still suffer from "math anxiety." It's a fact that seven out of ten girls' math grades begin a steep decline in middle school. Since many of us equate math with finances, the impact of this math anxiety on our ability to make and manage money is profound. Thankfully, it's also reversible.

According to Lori Sackler, author of *The M Word: The Money Talk Every Family Needs to Have About Wealth and Their Financial Future,* another factor is based in gender. "Women and men think about and manage money differently," says Lori. "Women tend to be more conservative and long-term in their planning and investing, much of it around family members. Men tend to take more risk and make short-term trading decisions. This can result in unexpected differences in returns and outcomes. Unfortunately, many of us still tend to defer to men to take control of our finances, which can be a mistake. Bottom line, women need to take charge of their finances."

Income Potential versus Income Reality

Fess up. Are finances just "not your thing"? Do you have lingering math anxiety that makes you feel you're not "good with numbers"? Did you grow up in humble surroundings and somehow acquire the mistaken belief that generating wealth is a shallow goal? If you answered "yes" to any of these questions, then it's time to assess your income potential versus your income reality. For now, what matters is not how much money you could or should be making. The question is how much money you *are* making. Our purpose is not to discuss investment strategies, but to persuade you to take responsibility for your financial affairs. This means knowing exactly where you stand in terms of monthly income, outstanding bills, projected income, and available savings.

30
REALIZE THAT OZZIE AND HARRIET ARE LONG GONE.

Women and girls have to own a part of the system—stocks, bonds, and a business—if we aren't going to be owned by it.

JOLINE GODFREY, BUSINESS EXECUTIVE AND WRITER (1950–)

Harriet Left the House Without Her Cash

We were in New York. Michealene had set up a meeting with her friend, Gerry Laybourne, the legendary woman who created the Nickelodeon network, brought Big Bird and Sesame Street to TV, and invented Nick at Nite. Gerry wanted to talk with us about the book we were writing, because she thought we might have some good stories for her new Oxygen Network, especially as they pertained to women and their finances.

We sat in Gerry's office and shared our financial ups and downs. Gerry listened intently. Then she told us—in the kindest way—that each of us was ultimately responsible for our financial state and that blaming our husbands for the mess we were in was unfair to them and less than brilliant on our part. We knew she was right. Although we were all educated, we were guilty of having "Ozzie and Harriet" mentalities when it came to money.

The 1950s TV sitcom *Ozzie and Harriet* exemplified traditional male and female roles decades ago. Harriet was the classic homemaker. She always seemed to be wearing an apron and wielding an iron with a loving smile on her face. Of course, homemade chocolate chip cookies were always ready for the kids when they came home from school.

Today, Harriet would be juggling a full-time job along with her homemaking responsibilities. She and Ozzie would both be commuting to work every day, swapping turns schlepping the kids to soccer, and divvying up chores on the weekend. Yet one thing hasn't changed. Many women are still delegating their family finances to their husbands.

THIS IS NOT THE LIFE I ORDERED

Far too many women still naïvely believe that the men in their lives were somehow magically born with the "money-management gene." Fathers, brothers, husbands, or business partners—women still trust them with their finances more than they trust themselves. Ladies, it's time for us to grow up.

"BAD TIME TO TALK MONEY?"

The first step toward growing up and taking responsibility for our financial health is to educate ourselves and start to understand the vocabulary of money. It's important to know about equity, debt, financial risk, and the types of instruments you can access. Do you read the financial or business section of the newspaper? No? It's time to start. Have you ever bought a copy of *Money Magazine* or, for a more challenging read, the *Wall Street Journal*? No? Throw an issue in your cart next time you go to the supermarket. Do you watch any of the investment shows on TV featuring investment experts? Yes? Good for you. No? Next time you're channel surfing and see Suze Orman, stop. Listen to her sage advice about the importance of clearing up that credit-card debt. You may even want to buy her audio series. It's a painless way to educate yourself about money while taking your morning walk, jogging on the treadmill, or driving to work. Jean Chatsky is another brilliant financial author who has written several books that can help you figure it all out.

We've all heard the adage: Knowledge is power. We believe that acting on knowledge is what produces power. You don't have to re-create the finance wheel. There are plenty of experts who will save you trial-and-terror learning if you just read their articles, listen to their broadcasts, or watch their shows. But it's up to you to act on their wisdom so that money becomes a vital part of your life instead of something you think about only at the end of the month when it's time to pay bills.

31
FOLLOW YOUR CASH SO IT DOESN'T END UP IN SOMEONE ELSE'S POCKET.

One of the most powerful determinants of a woman's quality of life is her relationship with money. If she takes good care of her financial health, she lives life on her terms.

CHERYL RICHARDSON, WRITER (1964–)

Women Have the Money Gene

When women choose to focus on making more money and managing it wisely, they can and do create financial miracles. Did you know that all-women investment clubs consistently earn more than all-men investment clubs? Women money-mangers (although there are still too few of them) tend to outperform their male counterparts. Melinda Evans, a veteran Wall Street trader, said: "Women have inherent female skills that give them an advantage in the investment world. For example, they usually do more research and are less impulsive about their investments. Men tend to be less patient, which means they jump in and out of the market more often, which can nullify any significant gains." We have the money gene—we just have to learn to use it!

Jane Williams has the money gene. She had a vision more than twenty years ago to help women build stronger financial futures, so she co-founded Sand Hill Global Advisors. Jane chose to focus her practice on helping women. Why? "Because it makes me feel good," she says, "and because I believe a financially competent woman is a powerful person who can change the world." Her company now manages several billion dollars in assets, and Jane was named one of the 100 most influential businesswomen in the Bay Area.

Jane and Emilie Goldman, chief wealth manager of Sand Hill Advisors, decided to form the Women's Wealth Network to "inspire, educate, and empower women to take charge of their financial lives." They help women who are going through transitions like divorce, the death of a spouse, or a career change to plan and execute their financial rebirth. Together with Lori Sackler of Morgan Stanley, they helped us to develop six steps for taking charge of your money. Six steps? Everyone, no matter how busy, can handle six steps!

1. *Learn your net worth*: Know what you own and what you owe. Begin by creating a net-worth statement. Compile the total value of your assets and subtract your debt. The remainder is your net worth. Emile recommends that women review their annual spending by going through their checkbook registries and credit-card statements to develop a written picture of where cash is going. Lori suggests entering the information into an electronic register like Quicken, an easy-to-use and powerful tool that can help you stay updated on your spending and saving. After you have a complete picture of your cash, begin to develop a budget and review it every three months. Gather up all life insurance, health insurance, and 401(k) and/or pension documents (which, if you are like many women, will be scattered in drawers through-out your house). Review these important documents and

note anything you don't understand. If you can't explain why you're paying a certain amount for coverage or what the policy means, start asking questions until you understand. Make copies of these documents and give them to a relative you can trust so they have a copy in case of emergency. Place the original documents in an accessible, fireproof file box and plan to review them annually to keep them current. (Please note: Every year, people learn how important these documents are when they have to evacuate their homes quickly due to a fast-approaching hurricane or wildfire. The frustrating and time-consuming efforts needed to replace these documents can also delay payment on your policies when you need the money most.)

2. ***Create a vision and an action plan***: After you have calculated your net worth and created a budget, it is time to create a vision for your financial future. This is as important as getting a mammogram. On average, however, we spend more time picking out a new pair of shoes than we do planning our financial futures. The financial vision you create will become your touchpoint for making all kinds of decisions. Set specific money-related goals. Do you want to buy a house? Start a business? Take a vacation? Create an emergency fund? Whatever it is, write it down and make sure it "lights your fire." If the vision doesn't inspire you, you won't have the willpower to sacrifice short-term gratification for long-term financial gain. When your vision is clearly articulated, write down the concrete steps you need to take in order to make it a reality. For example, if your vision is to pay college tuition for your daughter, how much do you need to acquire in loans and grants along with saved cash? If your vision includes starting a business, where will you find seed money or partners?

3. ***Educate yourself***: We all need to learn the language of finance. Every discipline, from medicine to raising

orchids, has its own language. Unfamiliar terms can make you feel dumb. Don't allow that discomfort to paralyze you. You don't have to be a day-trader to understand concepts like mutual funds, bull markets, and S-corporations. Take a class at your local community center or begin an adult education program. Visit a financial website and read the many free articles available online. Seek out a mentor who is financially successful and ask her for her best lessons on how you can start creating wealth.

4. ***Take advantage of company tools and stock options***: If you work for a company, have monthly allotments deducted from your pay and put directly into some type of 401(k) account that helps you save instead of spend. If you build that amount into your monthly budget, you won't miss it. Commit bonuses, certain commissions, raises, and tax refunds to a savings account or money-market account.

5. ***Engage support***: The financial world is complicated. When we're faced with a medical crisis, we seek the best medical advice from the best doctors. Why not do the same for your finances? Lori lists the different professionals we can connect with depending on the transition we're facing—experts like financial advisors or planners, insurance professionals, attorneys, accountants, mental-health professionals, or care managers if you have a family member suffering from a long-term illness. "It is difficult and unwise to make important financial decisions without some type of input from outside resources," she warns, "as the opportunities for errors are considerable."

6. ***Have the "Money Talk"***: Lori suggests having a money talk with family members who are impacted by our decisions and our "money transitions." "Talking about money is a big taboo in many cultures," she says. "But we need to start talking if we are going to successfully navigate difficult transitions." There is a 70 percent failure rate in

transferring assets from one generation to the next, and the major reason for this is a break-down in communication and trust. Every transition is challenging—whether death, divorce, changing jobs, caring for an aging parent, or retirement. Unless we have conversations with our spouses, partners, children, and others who are impacted, we may find unexpected challenges and roadblocks along the way.

PENALTY SIGNALS FOR FINANCIAL MISMANAGEMENT

ROUGHING
THE WALLET

IN OVER
YOUR HEAD

FAILURE
TO SAVE

FILING FOR
CHAPTER II
(BANKRUPTCY)

LOST SHIRT,
NO RESERVES

CHOKING ON
MONTHLY
PAYMENTS

BAD
RECORD
KEEPING

LACK OF
SMARTS

STINKY
INVESTMENT

THIS IS NOT THE LIFE I ORDERED

And let's not forget taxes. Taxes, like death, are a certainty. All women should understand their tax returns. Don't just sign them! If someone prepares the return for you, understand that it is your right and responsibility to ask questions so you know exactly why you're claiming items, why you can't deduct items, and why you need to file a particular type of form. If the person preparing your taxes seems impatient or unable to answer your questions, find someone who understands that part of his or her job is to explain this process so you are comfortable with it.

Deal with the Big When It Is Small

Barbara Stanny, the daughter of the "R" in H&R Block, is an expert on women and money who has helped millions take charge of their finances. She wasn't always that savvy, however.

Barbara grew up believing that her father would take care of her, which he did. She then thought she would marry and her husband would take care of her. She married, had children, and assumed her husband was managing her money, until she experienced an unexpected and defining moment at an ATM. She tried to withdraw some cash, but her account registered "insufficient funds." How could that be? Imagine her shock when she discovered that her husband had gambled all her money away! In what Barbara describes as a devastating but ultimately welcome wake-up call, she began a journey toward economic enlightenment. Barbara wrote a best-selling book entitled *Prince Charming Isn't Coming: How Women Get Smart About Their Money*, which we highly recommend. Barbara believes there are two fundamental truths regarding women and money.

1. You don't need thousands of dollars to begin implementing successful financial strategies. Barbara has witnessed teachers, bookkeepers, stay-at-home moms, and others who didn't have a "big wad of cash" build a sizeable net worth using her techniques.

2. Don't wait until a crisis to get started. Barbara warns that too many women ignore their finances until an emergency forces them into action. Don't wait for something to go wrong to get smart about money. All it takes is a decision on your part to "deal with the big while it is still small."

We all wish we had met Barbara, Lori, Jane, and Emilie earlier in our lives. Their wise advice could have saved us a lot of heartache. But it's not too late for you. We have included several tools in the next WIT Kit that can help you take charge of your finances—starting today. Please don't delay. These straightforward steps are doable, and they could make the difference between you and your loved ones living the lives you deserve or wondering how you're going to pay next month's rent.

WIT KIT TOOLS FOR UNDERSTANDING MONEY

1. Schedule a half-day of your life to organize and update your finances. Instead of viewing this exercise with dread, pat yourself on the back and give yourself credit for taking responsibility for facing your financial facts. By taking the time to inform yourself about the reality of your financial worth, you are putting naïveté behind you and acting like the adult you are.

2. Gather all your financial documents. That includes insurance policies, checking and savings statements, investment account statements, mortgage papers, credit-card bills, alimony receipts, and so on. Remember the equation:

   All that you own – All that you owe = Your net worth

   Develop a clear statement of outstanding debts versus the current and projected costs of your financial vision. Create an action plan and write out your timeline and

THIS IS NOT THE LIFE I ORDERED

monetary plans for your retirement or any other goal you may want to achieve. What will you be doing? Where will you be living? How much will it cost? Are you setting aside sufficient funds (taking inflation into account) so you will have enough money to take care of yourself in the later stages of life?

3. Take out your WIT Kit journal and craft your financial vision. Make your words sing back to you on the page. Remember Emilie Goodman's and Lori Sackler's advice: Create a financial vision so compelling and personally meaningful that it motivates you to pass up tempting but less important purchases in order to save for your top priorities.

4. Make finances the topic of an upcoming kitchen-table group. Talk about the financial challenges you each face and brainstorm about how all of you can get smarter about money. Discuss beliefs regarding money that you may still be carrying around from childhood. Plan how you can all "grow up" and start valuing yourselves enough to charge what you're worth and demand salaries commensurate with your talents.

5. If you are a widow, make sure you apply for a widow's benefit through Social Security. If you are a widow and have turned sixty, you can qualify for a widow's benefit and defer your own benefit until age seventy. This strategy allows your benefit to grow much larger.

6. You don't need to be wealthy to make an appointment with a financial planner or advisor. Make the appointment or invite an advisor to your kitchen-table group. Join a group or visit a website like *Ellevate*, started by Sallie Krawcheck, that can provide you with good information and tools to help with your financial goals.

CHAPTER FIVE

WHEN LIFE IS NOT WHAT YOU ORDERED, BEGIN AGAIN

New beginnings are often disguised as painful endings.

**LAO TZU,
CHINESE PHILOSOPHER**

32
NEVER SAY NEVER.

Many of our life crises are divinely scheduled to get us to change and head in a different direction.

CAROLINE MYSS, MEDICAL INTUITIVE AND WRITER (1952–)

Change Is Messy

The four of us have come to know change as an irrevocable aspect of the human condition. For too long, we used every bit of our energy to maintain the status quo. But, just when we thought we had experienced enough transitions for a lifetime, change visited us again.

Change, whether welcomed or forced, can be messy and unpredictable. It forces us to reexamine what we thought we knew, what we thought we could count on. Change dices, slices, and cuts to the core of our being. We finally learned to surrender our Quixotic battle against change and embrace it. So how do you make change a welcome partner instead of a dreaded plague? You begin by developing a new attitude toward it.

Have you ever taken one of those stress quizzes that ask you about the big changes in your life? The higher your total score, the higher your risk for a stress-related illness. When Jan took it, she tested off the charts!

"I was forty-seven when John died," Jan recollects. "Many people asked me if I would marry again. Never! I replied—and I meant it. Then I met Rob on a blind date, and eight and a half months later—you guessed it—we were married. Later, we divorced. I will never say 'never' again."

Before Rob and Jan married, she put her home up for sale thinking it would take months to sell. Much to her surprise, she accepted an offer before she even had an open house. It was a cash offer, with a contingency that she close and move within thirty days. She took the offer, packed up the furniture and sent it to storage, and sent the dog to the grandparents. Then she took her three kids and the babysitter and moved into a hotel for two months.

"In less than ten years," Jan marvels, "I had buried one husband, married another, sold a home, moved across two counties, enrolled my kids in three new schools, became a stepmother to two teenagers, and then divorced. I inherited two dogs, one cat, and a dozen koi fish, and I started a new job. Change became my steadfast companion. And I've learned that, no matter how messy it is, you have to look change squarely in the eye and embrace it with gusto!"

To deal with the overwhelming changes in her life, Jan embraced a process that has served her well. She gave up searching for "whys"—Why did he die? Why did I get breast cancer? Why didn't I save money? Why did he leave?—and started embracing "hows." "There are great mysteries in life that I will never completely understand," she admits, "so I choose to focus on 'how.' I look for 'how' everywhere. I ask: How can I make what happened work in our lives? How can we move forward? How can I help? While I don't think we can completely rid ourselves of the 'whys,' I simply prefer 'hows.' They empower me and give me a proactive attitude."

The Power of Words

Attitude is not something we are born with. That's good news, because it means we can shape it in ways that help instead of hinder. In fact, your attitude is the only element in your life over which you have total control. In our experience, the most powerful way to shape your attitude is to choose your words carefully when you talk to others and to yourself. Our words—whether spoken, written, or thought in private—impact how we view the world and ourselves. The words we choose and the questions we ask either support us or sabotage us. Words either fill us with confidence or cause us to retreat in defeat.

You are in charge. You can choose to use words to describe a job loss as a crisis or as an opportunity to move into a more rewarding career. You can describe a divorce as a personal failure or as a needed wake-up call. You can conclude that a financial setback is permanent or purely temporary. The language you use paints word pictures that become your reality.

Over the years, we have learned to rely on a series of questions to shape our "first response" to life-changing events. These questions help us stay focused on constructive responses instead of panicky reactions. They bring focus to what we *can* do instead of what we cannot.

- ***What's the good news in this situation?*** The question itself tells your mind that there is a positive side just waiting to be uncovered and expressed. It focuses your mental energy on finding an optimistic instead of a pessimistic interpretation.

- *What actions can I take that will benefit all involved?* This question reminds you that, while you may not be able to control what's happened, you do control how you respond to what's happened. It helps you to concentrate on actions that serve all involved instead of wallowing in how unfair or undeserved the situation may be.

- *Who (or what) can help me out in this situation?* This question helps you remember that you are never alone. The world is filled with people who can help you resolve issues. You simply need to find them and ask.

Are you facing something daunting in your life right now? Take a few moments to answer these three questions in your WIT Kit journal. They can help you move from a "Woe is me" reaction to a "What can I do?" response.

Persist; Don't Retreat

Billie Dragoo was named by *Fortune* magazine as one of the top women entrepreneurs in the nation. She serves as CEO of the Indianapolis-based RepuCare, one of the fastest-growing companies in the United States. Billie started RepuCare as a single mom with two young children. She exemplifies the practice of turning "woe is me" into action.

"I simply refuse to give up," Billie says. "I saw giving up as a luxury I couldn't afford." Billie grew up in a dysfunctional environment with little parental support. She claims she was lucky she even graduated from high school. Married at a young age and then divorced, she was ostracized by others in the small Midwestern town where she lived. Yet, she had a dream for herself and her children. "I was working for an executive search firm and I became a top agent. It occurred to me that this company was making a lot of money from the work I was doing. I decided I wanted a bigger share of the money, so at night, I went to the library to research how to start my own business." When her kids were sleeping, Billie studied.

"I took the leap and never looked back," Billie recalls. "There were several times when I came close to bankruptcy and had to rebuild. When I finally thought I had made it, the CFO I had hired and implicitly trusted suddenly died. I also discovered that an employee had embezzled a lot of my money! Even during those bad times, however, I truly have never been depressed a day in my life. I think that's why I've been able to persist instead of retreat. I never could afford to get depressed! I refuse to let myself go to a dark place. I just wake up every day and do something in pursuit of what I want and I keep my mind away from what I don't want."

Billie's lack of a "woe is me" attitude accompanied her as Chairwoman of the National Association of Women Business Owners (NAWBO), where she spoke "loudly and clearly" to the President of the United States, business leaders, and even Warren Buffett on the importance of women entrepreneurs to the economy. She said: "I've been to so many meetings over the past several years and each time we walk away with good feelings and no action. Gentlemen, I'm tired of hearing how important we women are when lack of investment dollars tells a different story. When are you actually going to quit talking and do something?" It was a moment of bravery. Billie said it was just a matter of her passion. "I had a rough road and I don't intend for other women to have to encounter what I lived through. So I'm not keeping quiet until things change. And I don't mean just lip service or nice speeches—I mean real change."

33
JUST SIT WITH IT.

The mind is like water. When it's turbulent, it's difficult to see. When it's calm, everything becomes clear.

**PEMA CHODRON, AMERICAN BUDDHIST
NUN AND AUTHOR (1936–)**

Deborah made an appointment with her doctor. "It's simple," she said. "I want to be able to know that whatever life throws at me, I can take it. Is that too much to ask?" Her doctor had a most unusual prescription—not a pill, but a pillow. A meditation pillow, to be exact. He urged her to enroll in the Mindfulness-based Stress Reduction (MBSR) program, an eight-week course that had taught him how to meditate. He said it had been life-changing for him.

"While I had heard of the positive effects of meditation," Deborah recounts, "hearing my Harvard-educated MD tell me that, in medical studies, meditation is as or more effective than anti-depressants encouraged me to give it a shot." The scientific evidence for meditation is overwhelming. It increases immune function and changes the gray matter in your brain in ways that may help prevent Alzheimer's. Meditation can significantly decrease pain in the body and inflammation at the cellular level. It decreases anxiety and stress, and increases positive emotions.

The program Deborah enrolled in (now offered around the world) was developed at the University of Massachusetts Medical Center by Jon Kabat-Zinn. The course has helped people with chronic pain, terminal illness, stress, and trauma, giving remarkable results. While participants are taught to meditate, they also learn about their behaviors, emotions, and habits, and the impact of these on their minds and bodies. The course helps them recognize and stop anxiety, and shows them how to identify patterns in their lives that are not helping, but hurting.

"Learning to 'sit' with difficult emotions and not allow them to overtake me was life-changing," Deborah claims. "I am increasingly more comfortable with uncertainty, for I've learned that all we really have is the present moment to think and react in ways that help or hurt us."

34
INVENT A SECRET
LANGUAGE FOR CHANGE.

Life is a process of becoming, a combination of states we have to go through. Where people fail is that they wish to elect a state and remain in it. This is a kind of death.

ANAÏS NIN, FRENCH WRITER (1903–1977)

Dreaded Questions

Seemingly innocent questions asked by colleagues during times of change can sometimes leave us depleted. It can be helpful to create responses in advance that you can use to answer those questions you dread.

After leaving a popular TV show that she'd hosted for fifteen years, Jan dreaded running into people because their well-intended, solicitous questions left her tongue-tied. "Being on television meant my face was broadcast into the homes of thousands of people. That was a wonderful gift, but it became a nightmare when the show was canceled. Everywhere I went, complete strangers would inevitably start the conversation with: 'So, Jan, what are you doing now?' I didn't want to go into a lengthy explanation, but there was no short answer to that question."

Jackie ended her term in the California legislature after a ten-year stint. "It was not my choice to leave. By law, I was limited to the number of years I could serve. The timing of my departure could not have been worse. I was a new widow with a two-year-old daughter and an eight-year-old son. As a public figure, I was often asked: 'What are your plans now?' It was a simple and appropriate question, yet I didn't know what to say."

THIS IS NOT THE LIFE I ORDERED

"IF YOU ASK ME, THAT WOMAN
WAS A LITTLE TOO HAPPY."

Michealene left a high-profile job to have children. "I opened up an office in my home and started my own company. I traded in my suits for blue jeans, and my work time was built around family time. I was always surprised to learn that few people thought I had a 'real job.' Countless times I was asked: 'So now that you are not working, what do you do?' It was as if I had become invisible because I had become a different kind of 'working mom.' I didn't know what to say."

When you are at a loss for words, you lose your power. If you're feeling like a fish out of water, in search of a way back to the pond, it's in your best interests to anticipate questions. Crafting answers for these awkward circumstances can help you anticipate and handle those moments with more wisdom and less panic. Dealing with the emotions that inevitably arise when you aren't sure of who you are anymore is also important. When corporate titles, executive offices, and powerful connections are suddenly gone, you may feel out of sorts and aimless. That's why it's important to use words consciously when talking to others and to yourself—words that make you feel in control rather than out of control.

Our Secret Language

We developed a secret language for these trying situations. It was an acquisition made of necessity, as we didn't have the luxury of hiding out. We had to get out of the house and network with people who had the power to direct us toward new futures. We had to verbalize what we wanted and how we were going to get it, instead of allowing ourselves to wallow in or express our concerns. We have tried out many phrases and have test-driven them through some rocky terrain. They gave us an aura of self-assurance that we may not have had otherwise. Perhaps one or more of these phrases will help you answer your own sensitive questions graciously and confidently:

- I'm taking a sabbatical. I'm exploring some opportunities and interests I've neglected for too long.

- I've given myself a time-out to recharge my batteries. I'll probably take time off to do something different and then resume my business (or job search).

- Remember the caterpillar and metamorphosis? Well, I'm in the cocoon stage, on my way to becoming something new. I'm excited!

- I'm in transition, taking time to choose my next path wisely.

- I'm being a kid again—learning, playing, exploring my options. I'll return to the adult world soon!

Are you in the middle of a transition and finding that people keep asking you well-meaning but embarrassing questions? Instead of allowing yourself to be tongue-tied, take the time to create and rehearse answers so you no longer have to dread running into people. Practice your answers in front of the mirror until you can say them with confidence.

If, for some reason, you can't come up with a satisfactory response, make this a topic for your next kitchen-table group. Talk about the delicate questions you dread and brainstorm possible replies so you don't have to worry about your mind going blank when asked: "So what's new?"

35
SAY THE UNSAYABLE.

I began to have an idea of life, not as a slow shaping of achievement to fit my preconceived purposes, but as the gradual discovery and growth of a purpose, which I did not know.

JOANNA FIELD, BRITISH PSYCHOLOGIST (1900–1986)

Speak Your Truth

We have found that one of the keys to welcoming change instead of running from it is to give ourselves permission to articulate what's going on in our guts, even when it isn't pretty or politically correct. This isn't just our discovery. Activist and author Gloria Steinem once said: "Every woman needs an outlet for saying the unsayable." Every woman needs to speak her truth.

One of the reasons we came together as friends was because we all needed a safe place to say our "unsayables." We desperately needed a place where we could say how we really felt without having to apologize for it or be embarrassed by it. In that forum, we were able to get out what we honestly thought, but didn't dare say out loud. We were free to express our most fragile feelings: I'm contemplating a divorce. I'm on the verge of bankruptcy. My husband is having an affair. I have a lump in my breast and I'm afraid it's cancer. My son is using drugs. I have lost my job.

An amazing thing happens when you are finally able to share the "ugly" truth about what's really happening in your world. Your friends offer sympathy and support so you don't have to shoulder that burden alone. You get it off your chest so you don't feel so weighed down and immobilized. Instead of it being a deep, dark secret you have to carry by yourself, it becomes something you see clearly and are empowered to face.

"HONEY, LET ME START BY SAYING THAT I, TOO, HAVE ANNOYING HABITS."

THIS IS NOT THE LIFE I ORDERED

We've come up with a few questions that bring out the "unsayables" so we can admit them and deal with them honestly:

- Do I live life in accordance with my standards? Yes? No? Why? What are those standards?

- Am I deeply satisfied with my life?

- How do I define success? Do I consider myself successful?

- What fills me up? What makes me feel that I am "enough" just the way I am? What keeps me from feeling that I'm "enough"?

- Am I living in the right place for me?

- Am I doing the right kind of work for me?

- Are my family relationships satisfying?

- Are my friendships satisfying?

- What level of "newness" do I need each week? What am I doing to bring that freshness into my life?

Make these questions a topic for your kitchen-table group. Instead of going around the table and alternating answers to each question, give each participant twenty to thirty minutes to talk through her answers to all these questions. Take advantage of this chance to explore your status quo fully to find out whether you're satisfied with it or yearning to make changes and just haven't had the clarity or courage to do things differently.

Agree up front to be completely honest. You can't improve anything if you don't first confess it is less than ideal. Once you have dared to tell the truth about your life, you can start planning how to make it better.

WIT KIT TOOLS FOR WHEN LIFE IS NOT WHAT YOU ORDERED

1. In your WIT Kit journal, label a page Changes I'd Like to Make. Start writing everything that comes to mind, whether it seems feasible or not. Remember, it doesn't have to make sense to anybody except you. Everything that occurs to you counts. If you think it, ink it.

2. Go back over that list and pick one "small" thing you can do this week and one "large" thing you can do by the end of the year. Plan exactly how you're going to accomplish the "small" thing you want to achieve by the end of the

THIS IS NOT THE LIFE I ORDERED

week. If you want to get back into morning walks with your friend, pick up the phone and call her right now to make a walking date for later this week.

3. Plan the first step to achieving your "large" change. What is one thing you can do this week to jump-start that change? Next, plan a series of small steps you can take each week to make that large change a reality.

4. Ask your kitchen-table group to hold you accountable for making your small change and for stepping toward your large change, so you consciously and proactively make change a part of your life.

CHAPTER SIX

REINVENTING YOURSELF

*I have found that life persists in the
midst of destruction and, therefore,
there must be a higher law than
that of destruction.*

**INDIRA GANDHI,
FORMER PRIME MINISTER
OF INDIA (1917–1984)**

36

RECOGNIZE THAT CHOCOLATE HAS TO MELT IN ORDER TO TAKE A NEW FORM.

I am not a has-been. I'm a will-be.

LAUREN BACALL, ACTRESS (1924–2014)

Melting Down

Let's admit it. Everyone has meltdowns. There are simply days that may appear totally devoid of hope. We call them "meltdown days"—a perfect description of when it seems as if your world has been turned upside down. These are the days when we don't know what to believe or whom we can trust. On these days, we remember that chocolate also has to melt—its entire substance has to change—before it can take on a new form. It is a perfect metaphor to remind you that, during the worst of times, when you've lost your "form," you can rebuild.

You awake on meltdown days wishing you didn't have to get out of bed. The world has become overwhelming. Events have stacked up to the point that you're not sure you can handle them. You feel scared and immobilized. What should you do? Give yourself permission to stay in bed for a day. Understand that your system is overloaded and needs to recuperate and recharge. Chances are that you have at least one or more sick days coming to you. Take one now. Get caught up on sleep. Resist the urge to do paperwork, chores, or other "responsible" stuff. For one day, gather strength by nurturing and indulging yourself.

Make yourself a promise. Tomorrow you will rise, greet the day, put on your best face, and move forward. You will go back out into the world, determined to "fight the good fight" with renewed energy and commitment. After you have replenished yourself, call someone who cares about you and ask if you can buy him or her lunch. During lunch, talk honestly about what you're going through and ask for advice about possible next steps. Also, get in touch with at least one professional "fan"—a former boss or colleague who is familiar with your qualifications—and brainstorm ways to get back on track personally and professionally.

Getting Back "In Play"

An important part of helping yourself take on a new form is to "be in play," even if you do not know what game you are playing. "In play" means being out of the house and deliberately visible in your local community and/or professional setting so people see you in action. Only when people have a chance to spend time with or around you will they initiate on your behalf. ("You know what? You'd be perfect for this job!")

We're speaking from experience. Each time we made ourselves get up and out and into life after indulging in one "personal day," things got better. Each time we forced ourselves back into play, something good happened as a result of that excursion.

SOMETIMES KAREN NEEDED A JUMPSTART.

Are you in the middle of a meltdown? Has it been increasingly tempting to stay home with the shades drawn? Have you been avoiding friends and playing "hermit"? Do you wish you could crawl under your covers and make the world go away? This lack of action—called "checking out"—is a form of denial. It is a slippery slope, because it becomes easier and easier to hide. But isolating ourselves only makes things worse, because we end up spending all our time inside the emotional hell of whatever situation we are experiencing. We lose perspective and feel more and more helpless. We get locked in inertia.

If this is how you've been feeling, resolve to put yourself back in play. Tell yourself you've had your quota of meltdown days and that it's time for you to assume your new form. Your new form requires you to get out of the house and reconnect with people who have the power to give you job leads, shore up your self-esteem, and suggest proactive next steps.

37
WHEN DREAMS TURN
TO DUST, VACUUM.

Hope is a thing with feathers.
That perches in the soul,
And sings the tune without the words,
And never stops at all.

EMILY DICKINSON, POET (1830–1886)

Reclaiming Hope

When dreams crumble, hope is the first thing lost, yet it is the most important thing we need to reclaim. Immediately, swiftly, and with a great sense of purpose, we must become hopeful and optimistic about the future. We have learned that, when dreams crumble, we must simply vacuum up the pieces, tossing aside what didn't work and using what did or could. It's called resilience, and Arlan Hamilton is the queen of resilience.

Glancing at her credentials, you might mistake Arlan Hamilton as part of Silicon Valley's cadre of elite technology executives. She is, in fact, the founder of Backstage Capital

Venture Fund. She was named by *Fortune* magazine as one of the top forty women in America and was recently hailed as the hottest venture capitalist in the United States. She has raised and invested millions of dollars in companies of which at least one founder is a woman, a person of color, or a member of the LGBT community. Recently, she announced a $36 million fund that will invest in black women entrepreneurs. Experts refer to it as a diversity fund, but Arlan calls it the "Its About Damned Time Fund!"

In order to truly understand the improbable rise of Arlan Hamilton, it's important to understand how the field is comprised. The venture capital industry is a potent combination of predominately white men with a ton of money flowing from family funds, new tech millionaires, and millions of dollars from public pension funds, hedge funds, and other elite institutional investors. Venture capitalists dole out billions of dollars to fledging entrepreneurs. Women, however, receive less than 3 percent of these funds. There are only a handful of women venture capitalists in the entire industry. Enter Arlan Hamilton, a black lesbian. Not hard to understand how the odds were stacked against her!

Two years before launching Backstage Capital, Arlan was sleeping on friends' couches, and even on the floor at San Francisco International Airport. Nearly broke and with no professional training in venture financing or funding, she had a dream of acquiring the millions to form a fund that should never have come true. But Arlan Hamilton was underestimated. She noticed that a lot of entertainment-industry personalities were investing in tech start-ups, and many were getting rich. So she used every spare moment to educate herself on the industry, while networking in creative ways with the influencers and gatekeepers. Those who know her say that it is her tenacity and her ability to rise in the face of numerous rejections that make her so remarkable.

Underestimated women like Arlan often rise to rule the world, but their journeys to power are rarely pleasant.

Charlotte Beers, the first woman CEO in America, said: "We are women and for that we will be tested. And in those tests, you need to know what you have inside that you can call on." Arlan Hamilton had a lot inside.

Women's talents, skills, and even intelligence are all too frequently underestimated. Sara Blakley, the founder of Spanx (and a billionaire, we might add), said that, in the pursuit of building her business, she was often underestimated and not taken seriously. A quick review of the successful women we know personally shows that most of them were underestimated. The stereotypes and assumptions that run rampant in our society create an unconscious bias against women before they even enter the room. Yet, we can use being underestimated as a sort of "superpower"!

38
DON'T TAKE THE CRUMBS; YOU'RE HERE FOR THE WHOLE CAKE.

Just like moons and like suns, with the certainty of the tides.
Just like hopes springing high, still I shall rise.

MAYA ANGELOU, AMERICAN POET (1928–2014)

When Arlan Hamilton was asked how she was able to pick herself up and dust herself off after being told "no" hundreds of times, she answered that she got her inspiration from a rap song lyric she heard one day: "I came for the cake, not the crumbs." "I didn't come here for just a little bit of it," she says. "I didn't come here to get your scraps. I didn't come here to get your pity or your charity. I came here to go toe-to-toe with you, head-to-head with you, and to take it all." Her answer is a lesson for all women in transition.

Settling or Choosing?

According to author Caroline Myss, there is a subtle difference between "settling" and "choosing." If you feel you settled for something, she claims, you can tell yourself you did so because of pressure or fear. In other words, you had no choice. "But your gut will never really let you off the truth-hook," she warns. "Making a choice, though more intimidating, puts you in the driver's seat of your own life and the consequences of each of your decisions."

"I was in my late twenties," Deborah remembers, "when Jackie Speier passed along advice that has never left me. She said sternly: 'Don't settle. Take the risk and go after what you want in life.' Over thirty-five years later, that advice is still with me. I've repeated it many times to my daughter, and to women leaders I work with. I still remind myself not to settle."

Right now, you may not be able to find one "good thing" in your life. You may think: Things are so bleak. I don't have anything to look forward to. Please trust us when we say that hope will help you open doors that now appear closed to you. In life-threatening situations, in times of crisis, when you are faced with the ugliest of circumstances, hope becomes a navigator that points you to a new place. It is the illuminator of paths and possibilities. Hope can help you get the whole cake and not settle for the crumbs.

This isn't just our opinion. Dr. Jerome Groopman, Harvard medical professor and author of *The Anatomy of Hope*, says:

> Hope does not arise from being told to think positively. Hope is the elevating feeling we experience when we see—in the mind's eye—a path to a better future. Hope gives us the courage to confront our circumstances and the capacity to surmount them. We are just beginning to appreciate the power of hope and have not defined its limits. I see hope as the very heart of healing.

Having hope doesn't mean being a Pollyanna. It means choosing—consciously deciding to look ahead and figure out exactly how you can transcend challenging circumstances by embarking upon a proactive, pragmatic plan of action.

"WELL, DOCTOR, EXCEPT FOR SOME DEEP-SEATED CONCERNS ABOUT MY HUSBAND, KIDS, AGING PARENTS, FRIENDS, MONEY, WORK, RACISM, MORAL VALUES, POVERTY, CANCER, AIDS, SEX, WAR, CRIME, THE ENVIRONMENT, PANDEMICS, SHADY POLITICIANS, GREED, THE GENERAL LACK OF CIVILITY, AND MY ONGOING BATTLES WITH FACIAL HAIR, EVERYTHING'S COOL, I GUESS."

That is what we mean by hope. Each of us has had dark, dark days. And each of us chose not to continue to live that way. We're not saying it was easy to get up and get on with our lives. We are saying that choosing to believe that there are better days ahead, and then taking action to ensure that there *are* better days ahead, is an option that is available to all of us.

So, what are you going to do today to look ahead with hope? What is one step you're going to take to make tomorrow better than today? Who is one person you're going to reach out to? What is one specific thing you are going to do to build, as Groopman says, "a path to a better future"?

If you're not sure what that could be right now, our next story will be particularly timely for you. It explains how the simple act of choosing to be grateful is one of the single best things you can do to make each day a better day.

39
BE GRATEFUL THE DOG DIDN'T PEE ON THE CARPET.

Don't block the blessings.

PATTI LABELLE, SINGER (1944–)

The Power of Gratitude

When we wrote about gratitude in our first book, not many knew of its remarkable powers. It's easy to ignore the positive influence of gratitude and to doubt its "healing" powers. When you're going through tough times, it can be hard to imagine that the simple act of feeling grateful can be such a life-changing tool. Recently, however, science has acknowledged the importance of gratitude to health and well-being. The cultivation of gratitude is now overwhelmingly recommended by psychotherapists, medical doctors, self-help gurus, and even the clergy as a way to endure adversity.

Beyond the improved well-being that is derived from gratitude, there are a host of other benefits that researchers have uncovered. We now know that grateful people have lower cortisol levels (related to stress) and tend to sleep better, especially when they think about what they are grateful for in the hour before falling asleep. Gratitude also boosts the immune system, which in turn creates more disease-fighting cells in your body. People who keep a gratitude journal have a reduced dietary fat intake—as much as 25 percent lower. Employing a daily gratitude practice can actually reduce the effects of aging on the brain.

Dr. Robert Emmons, professor of psychology at the University of California, whom we interviewed for our first book, has become a worldwide expert on the science of gratitude. He found that those who wrote in gratitude journals on a weekly basis also exercised more regularly, reported fewer physical symptoms, felt better about their lives, and were more optimistic than the control group that did not keep the journals. Participants who kept gratitude lists were more likely to have made progress toward important personal goals over a two-month period compared to those who did not. Dr. Emmons came to the conclusion that grateful people reported higher levels of positive emotions and lower levels of depression and stress.

NANCY CHANGED HER ATTITUDE JUST BEFORE WORK

Gratitude as a Healing Force

Deborah experienced the healing force of gratitude first-hand while dealing with her husband's terminal illness. "Our days were packed with doctor appointments, medical procedures, and unending stress," she relates. "I was afraid that the stress was beginning to affect our two young children, so I searched for anything that would pull me out of my sadness. A friend had given me a copy of a book called *Simple Abundance* by Sarah Ban Breathnach. One night, when I couldn't sleep, I opened the book and there it was staring back at me—the steps to creating a gratitude journal. I remember wondering what I had to be grateful for. My husband was dying and my life was falling apart. I did not have much respect for the concept of gratitude, but in desperation I decided to try it."

Deborah's first few attempts at gratitude were not successful. Yet, each night, after everyone had gone to bed, she sat in her favorite chair and wrote all that she had to be grateful for into a journal. "My entries were pitiful!" she recalls. "I wrote things like: I am grateful that the puppy didn't pee on the carpet today! I am grateful that we did not make a visit to the emergency room tonight."

She kept up this practice for nearly two weeks, forcing herself to write down at least two things she was grateful for. As she did, her ability to recognize the good things in her life grew. Miraculously, she started feeling better. "I cannot explain why it works," she admits. "I just know it does.

"Cultivating gratitude in your daily life is almost magical," Deborah now says. "It affects your sense of well-being and makes you stronger. I remember waking up in the morning feeling rested and not sad. My husband's doctors even mentioned to me that they thought I had a remarkable spirit! I literally went from a helpless wreck to a serene and positive woman in a matter of weeks. My circumstances had not changed, but I had. Now, my gratitude journal is my first line of self-defense when events in my life become crazy. I have immense respect for its power."

A Pearl of Gratefulness

When you are in the midst of a full-fledged crisis, identifying and cultivating gratitude may seem impossible, but Judy Sakaki's story may just be the motivation you need to get started. Judy is grateful to the woman who gave her socks as she and her husband fled their home barefoot from a wildfire. She is grateful to the man who gave her husband a t-shirt that day because he had none. All they had left was their lives.

"For miles in every direction, everything was burning," Judy says. "We were surrounded by flames and our feet blistered from the smoldering pavement. We were running and breathing smoke. We stumbled, carrying and supporting one another. I remember my husband telling me: 'We are going to get through this.' After walking several hundred feet, however, we both began to question whether we would die in the midst of an inferno. Suddenly, from among the dark smoke, lights emerged." And Judy is grateful for the firefighter who found them as he took a final pass through their neighborhood.

One month before telling this story of her gratefulness on a panel Jan had convened for the US-Japanese Council Conference in Washington, DC, Judy, the President of Sonoma State University and the first Asian woman to preside over a four-year university, had lost everything. As the deadly fires that swept California's wine country engulfed her house, she and her husband didn't even have time to grab their glasses. They ran for their lives in a frantic near-death escape. Nonetheless, she told the audience that, after losing everything, she feels only gratitude for those first responders.

While Judy and her husband were building their lives in Sonoma, Jane Yonamine was raising her three children and making annual trips to Hawaii to fill family and friends' requests for pearls. Through every purchase, she learned about pearls and developed an expert eye for quality and prices. In 1963, Jane decided to turn her "hobby" into a business. Armed with an entrepreneurial savvy that had evolved from her teenage years managing a soda fountain, Jane founded Yonamine Pearls. Her pearl necklaces became legendary and were coveted by Hollywood actresses, sports figures, and even the Vatican!

Judy Sakaki had a prized Yonamine pearl necklace that was lost in the fire that destroyed her home and she mentioned her loss the day she spoke on Jan's panel. Yonamine's granddaughter, Lynda, who just happened to be in the audience, stood up and removed the beautiful set of grey pearls she was wearing. She gave them to Judy as a contribution toward rebuilding her life and home.

A pearl forms when an irritant like a grain of sand attacks the heart of an oyster. In defense, the oyster exudes a viscous fluid to coat the irritant, depositing layer upon layer until a lustrous pearl is formed. Cultivating gratitude happens in a similar way. When we search for the "pearl of gratefulness" in the midst of disruptions, irritants, and loss, we enrich our lives and ensure our well-being. This is the powerful lesson we can learn from Judy Sakaki and Jane Yonamine.

So how do you go about searching for that pearl of gratefulness? You can begin by taking stock in a very simple way. What are you most thankful for today? Perhaps a friend has the uncanny knack of calling right when you need to talk to someone. Perhaps you have a loyal pet that sensed your mood and came over and nestled in your lap. Or maybe you are just thankful for your five senses—that you can walk and breathe and smell and see. Whatever it is that makes you grateful, start by identifying and acknowledging it.

Are you skeptical? Why not try it? Tomorrow morning, if you wake up and don't feel like facing the day, simply lie in bed and count all the things you have to be grateful for. Discover for yourself the power of choosing to focus on what's right with your world instead of what's wrong.

40
DON'T COMPLAIN; CREATE.

I was always looking outside myself for strength and confidence, but it comes from within. It is there all of the time.

ANNA FREUD, AUSTRIAN PSYCHOTHERAPIST AND DAUGHTER OF SIGMUND FREUD (1895–1982)

Rising from the Ashes

Neuroscientists have discovered that complaining changes our brains—and not in a good way. Neurons are special cells in the brain that send information throughout the body; they remember thought patterns and cause our bodies to respond appropriately. Complaining activates neurons that repeat our negative responses, causing them to be memorized by our brains and bodies. Over time, complaining physically entraps us and turns our world dark and hopeless. Women who are able to create instead of complain lead happier lives, because the act of creation changes their neurons and overrides the complaints lodged in their brains. Creation takes us away from negativity and into the world of possibility. Take, for example, the stories of Kathryn Tunstall and Marta Blodgett.

Kathryn was diagnosed with stage 2C breast cancer and given a 50 percent chance of surviving for five years. She underwent a lumpectomy and elected to do both chemotherapy and radiation. Eighteen months later, the cancer returned and she underwent a double mastectomy. At the time of her first diagnosis, Kathryn's two children were ages twelve and seven. As an executive of a medical-device company, Kathryn began to use her knowledge of the medical industry to search for clinical trials that might improve her odds of survival.

"There must be a better method to link patients like me with potentially life-saving clinical trials," Kathryn thought. She began to search for people who could help her. Applying her business skills to the most important project she would ever undertake, Kathryn assembled a team to save her own life and also offer hope to other people with life-threatening illnesses. Speaking from her hospital bed, Kathryn told us: "I realized that there was an opportunity to meet the needs of patients and to provide better information to make better decisions." So she launched Hopelink, a health-care solutions company, and raised the first round of funding of around $3 million. Many people join support groups when they face life-threatening illnesses. Kathryn started a company. Hopelink has helped thousands of patients facing life-threatening illnesses find and enroll in FDA-sanctioned clinical trials.

Marta McGinnis Blodgett sat in the cold waiting room of a hospital with some yarn and knitting needles to pass the time as she waited for chemotherapy treatments. She was shivering. She thought that no woman should shiver and be alone while undergoing treatment for cancer. As she knitted, she decided to create a blanket that she could pass along to the next woman who followed in her path. Thus Knit for a Cure was born. Marta and her friend teamed up with the largest wool manufacturer in America and inspired groups of women throughout the country to knit for a cause. The beautiful and warm hats, shawls, and blankets these women have knitted are now donated to cancer treatment centers across the country.

Women like Kathryn and Marta inspire us to take a shattered life and turn the experience into something that helps others while also helping ourselves. Mothers Against Drunk Driving was formed due to the death of Candy Lightner's daughter at the hands of a drunk driver. Shannon Watts, a mother of five, channeled her anger and grief after the Sandy Hook Elementary shootings to create Mom's Demand Action for Gun Sense in America. Tarana Burke is an African-American activist who founded the MeToo movement to bring attention to the pervasiveness of sexual assault in our society. Take their inspiring examples as a reason to go and do something about your own situation. You don't have to save the world. You only have to save yourself.

WIT KIT TOOLS FOR
REINVENTING YOURSELF

1. In your WIT Kit journal, label a page I Am Grateful for . . . and start free-associating and writing down everything that comes to mind. If your mind stalls after a few items, look around the room and start noticing things you appreciate.

2. Each night before you go to bed, write down three more things in your life you are grateful for. Even on bad days, force yourself to find at least three things. The very practice of looking for things for which to be grateful helps you develop a "grateful outlook," through which you start noticing the many other things in your life that are going right. Adding these entries to your journal every night makes being grateful a habit and helps you cultivate a mind-set of gratitude.

3. Begin writing a collection of letters to your children, your spouse, and people who are important in your life. Tell them what you are going through, how you are feeling, and what you have done to attempt to cope. Then seal the letters. Don't send them yet. After you have successfully managed the transition you wrote about, reread the letters. Write the ending to the story and share your lessons learned. Then you can decide whether you want to share your journey with the special people to whom you wrote.

4. Become an artist—yes, we mean you! Draw, paint, make over a room, plant a flower garden, do your best rendition of Georgia O'Keeffe. Lose yourself in expression and, for the moment, forget your problems. The exercise will refresh you and make you stronger.

CHAPTER 7

CARRYING WHAT CANNOT BE FIXED

*Taking action is an
antidote to despair.*

**JOAN BAEZ,
FOLK SINGER (1941–)**

THE CLUB NO ONE
WISHED TO JOIN

*Some things in life cannot be fixed. They can only
be carried.*

**MEGAN DEVINE, AMERICAN PSYCHOTHERAPIST
AND AUTHOR (1970–)**

Indoctrinated into widowhood—the club no woman wishes to join.
Deborah received two phone calls within minutes of her husband's
death. "First was Jackie. While I don't recall her exact words, I remember feeling so comforted, as she truly understood what I was going
through. Jan called me next. I gathered strength from her words, as
Jan had been exactly where I was in that moment. She gave me some
advice on comforting my children. She also arranged for us to stay
in her condo in Hawaii. She said it would be healing. It was such a
kind and generous act. How lucky I was to have these two women
in my life."

Since Jackie and Jan's entry into widowhood, the medical community understands much more about grief and its impact upon
those left behind. So many women like Jackie and Jan were often left
to figure things out on their own through a trial-by-fire effort. Today,
we know that grief is something that we can't overcome. All we can
really do is learn to carry it. One of the leading authorities on grief,
psychologist Megan Devine, says that society wants grieving people
to return to "normal" as quickly as possible. Megan demonstrates in
her research—and says in her book *It's OK that You're Not OK: Meeting
Grief and Loss in a Culture that Doesn't Understand*—that normal is
never going to happen. It will be a new sort of normal, but there will
never be a returning to what was.

As Megan states: "We are changed by our new realities. We
exist at the edge of becoming. We don't return to normal. That is
an impossible request. . . . There are whole lifetimes buried beneath
what now appears beautiful. We walk on the skin of ruins." What
follows are some of the lessons we've learned on walking through
widowhood.

41
LAUGH IN THE DARK.

What saved me was my sense of humor and the fact that I had a good literary education.

ERICA JONG, WRITER (1942–)

When her husband died, Jackie's mind and body needed to rest. She found herself dreaming of going to Hawaii. That was the place where she had always found a sense of physical and spiritual renewal. But such a trip would be impossible now. She was burying her husband tomorrow. Yet, the dream of fleeing to Hawaii with her young son and her unborn baby comforted her.

Almost out of the blue, a tiny voice piped up in her head: "Jackie, you have to pay for the funeral expenses. Charge them to your airline credit card. After the baby is born, the three of you can take the free miles and go to Hawaii." At first, the thought seemed almost disrespectful. Turning headstone costs into airline miles? What would the neighbors think?

But that is exactly what Jackie did. She realized that she couldn't bring her husband back, but she could take her children on a well-deserved vacation to a beautiful spot where they could reconnect in this trying time. So she paid for funeral expenses (including the headstone), programs, flowers, and a burial plot with her airline credit card.

Later on, Jan went through the same thought process and made a similar decision when faced with the expenses that lingered after her husband's death. "People don't realize that funerals cost a lot of money. I earned about 20,000 airline miles by charging all the funeral expenses. I always felt John would have been proud of me. He was a CPA, after all, and believed in using money wisely! I think he would have wanted me to take a trip with the kids after his death."

At first blush, the idea seems like the kind of dark humor only other widows would understand. Yet, we all have realized that dark humor is better than no humor. In fact, we have taught ourselves to laugh in the dark moments of our lives.

Remember earlier in the book when we talked about Norman Cousins's research into the healing power of humor? In our experience with traumatic transitions, we have discovered it's crucial to match the tears we shed with an equal number of laughs. When you're going through dark times, it's natural to see dark humor everywhere, the kind that only another person who's been in that type of crisis can laugh at. Most of the time, this involves looking at life and its moments with a critical eye for the funny, the absurd, and the hilarious. Take, for example, the friends gathered at Jackie's house after the death of her husband. One friend said: "Jackie is a very lucky person to have so many friends." Another friend (Katy) said: "Lucky isn't a word I'd use to describe Jackie. After all, she's been shot up and left for dead, and now she's three months pregnant and a widow! If that's luck, I don't want to be lucky."

Are you on the verge of taking yourself and your circumstances too seriously? Do you think it's disrespectful to enjoy yourself in the middle of a sad event? Try turning this belief around and realizing that dark humor is better than no humor. You may realize that having a good belly laugh just might be the most therapeutic thing you can do for yourself.

Keep your eyes and ears open for the absurd in what's happening to you. Don't be afraid to laugh. It's not wrong; it's one of the healthiest things you can do.

42

FORM A MERRY WIDOWS CLUB.

Maybe you have to know the darkness before you can appreciate the light.

MADELEINE L'ENGLE, AMERICAN AUTHOR (1918–2007)

Walking on the Skin of Ruins

There are times when women have to single-handedly invent their own help. Jackie and Jan did just that. Both had become widows with young children within a year of each other. They banded together to navigate the unknown challenges of single parenthood, death, financial tragedies, "dating," and work. They shared their fears and dreams. They helped each other cope with the loss of a spouse on a daily basis. Jackie and Jan called their bond "The Merry Widows Club."

"Our husbands' gravesites are about thirty yards apart," said Jan. "Father's Day was always difficult to get through, so we decided to have a picnic at the gravesites to celebrate it. We brought fried chicken, salad, and soft drinks, and my daughters, age eleven and thirteen at the time, brought their boom box. Our boys, ages six and seven, brought a baseball and bat. Stephanie, age ten months, watched as the boys used the grave markers as bases—we didn't think our husbands would mind."

Since then, this Merry Widows Club has expanded in membership. Whenever Jackie and Jan learn that a woman in the Bay Area has suffered the loss of a spouse, they contact her and extend their hands in support. They help new widows maneuver through funeral arrangements. They orchestrate food brigades for months at a time so a new widow does not have to worry about cooking for a family. They have organized health teams, car pools, and finance teams to deal with the details that can be overwhelming to widows during their time of grief.

The Merry Widows gather every few months to talk, support, learn, cajole, advise, find out who is dating, and search for hope. Jan says: "They are such a comfort to me. Sometimes we speak about our lost spouses with laughter. Someone who hasn't gone through this experience wouldn't understand. At one lunch, we talked about what we put in the coffins. I put in a deck of cards and letters from the children and myself. Another woman put in her husband's cell phone. She actually called it! Another time we asked each other if our husbands would have remarried if we had died. Every widow answered with a resounding 'Yes!' One widow said: 'The next month!' Now that some of us have remarried, we call ourselves the Merry and Married Widows Club."

In this kind of supportive community, we learn the lesson of commonality. If you are going through something alone, it's easy to think you're the only one who has ever gone through it. But when you talk with people who have experienced the same type of trauma, you discover that others have felt the same way you do and have thought the same thoughts. Your isolation turns into connection.

Commonality is a minute away on your computer. Google whatever it is you're dealing with (the loss of a child, divorce, bankruptcy, getting fired) and you'll find websites with support groups and chat rooms where you can connect with others to share the lessons they have learned and draw encouragement.

43
BUILD YOUR OWN
"KITCHEN CABINET."

So life changes and you have to change too. I don't like change, but I've learned you just put your hands over your eyes and step off the edge.

LINDA RONSTADT, SINGER (1946–)

Help Is a Gift—You're Worth It
One crisp winter morning, Jackie awoke determined to accept the help of those who had extended a hand to her

after the death of her husband. It was a difficult decision to make, as she was accustomed to being the strong one at the table, the one who did the giving but not the receiving. But she needed a sound plan for dealing with the very big issues her husband's death had created.

Methodically, she went through her list of acquaintances and found an accountant, a lawyer, a tax adviser, a real estate agent, and a banker. She invited them all to her home for a breakfast. Around her dining room table, this remarkable group of helpers assisted Jackie in devising a sound plan of action. This "kitchen cabinet" of friends left her home feeling gratified that they could contribute their expertise and their friendship to someone in need, while Jackie benefitted from their advice.

Help can come in many forms, from friends or from complete strangers who enter our lives in surprising ways. The first step is to be open to the fact that help is a gift you deserve. So the next time friends or acquaintances ask you if there is anything they can do, answer "Yes" and make a request. To prepare you for your next encounter with these potential helpers, complete this short exercise in your WIT Kit journal:

1. Identify the people who have offered to help you. What can they help you with? Make a list—for example, tax advice, referrals to a good lawyer, child care, someone to call when you're scared, steps to take, introductions to connections.

2. Now think about why you cannot ask for help or why you resist it. List all of your reasons—for example: It would be a burden. I'm afraid. What if they say no? I'll look foolish or weak when I am supposed to be strong. People will think I'm crazy!

3. Review your reasons and ask for help anyway. You have much to gain and very little to lose. And after you have asked and they say "yes," graciously receive their offer of help, simply accept it, and give a heartfelt "Thank you."

44
ASK FOR HELP.

My ancestors wandered in the wilderness for forty years, because even in biblical times, men would not stop to ask for directions.

BETTE MIDLER, COMEDIAN, ACTRESS, AND SINGER (1945–)

Don't Power On and Manage Through

As women, we are the first to give help and the last to ask for it. As mothers, daughters, wives, and business executives, we form the front line for caregiving. Yet, who cares for the caregiver? Numerous people can help, but we have to let them know that we need it. Sounds simplistic, but knowing when and whom to ask for help and graciously accepting it are among the most difficult things a woman has to learn.

Looking back, we can now spot the signs that we needed help. Yet, because we each had a strong tendency to power on and manage through, we convinced ourselves that if we just worked a little harder—adopted a new strategy, made a new connection—we could power through and manage our crisis and the chaos it brought just like any other project!

"I GOOGLED 'ENTITLED TEEN' AND 'MENOPAUSAL MOM' AND IT DOESN'T LOOK PRETTY."

THIS IS NOT THE LIFE I ORDERED

The laundry alone should have been our clue—it was piled so high we could not get into the laundry room! If you are lucky, you have a good friend who checks in daily to see how you are doing. If you are really lucky, that good friend secretly conspires to arrange for you to see a therapist who is good at helping people living during trying times.

Recognizing the first signs of distress can be difficult for women. We live in a culture where distress is often equated with weakness, so we try to hide it from the world and sometimes from ourselves. But when we are reluctant to admit our human frailties, it makes for a much more difficult journey than is necessary. The following are some signs that it's time to say "Help!"

- Your thinking isn't clear (and it's not related to hot flashes or a lack of protein in your diet).

- It is difficult for you to take action—the clothes you usually take to the cleaners are piled high in your closet, your son has no clean underwear, and your boss asks you if everything is okay.

- Inside, you feel like an orphan in a strange land. Everything you took for granted is up for grabs. Instead of waking up to greet the day, you pray that you can just get through the day.

- You are either eating too much, or you are forgetting to eat, or the stuff that you are eating is the kind of fast-food you swore you would never allow your children to have.

- People constantly talk to you about the light at the end of the tunnel. And when they say it, you silently scream: "I didn't want to be in the tunnel in the first place, so how far away from the light am I, and how the hell do I get out of here?"

- You have received multiple copies of the book *When Bad Things Happen to Good People* from friends and co-workers.

45
CHANGE YOUR ENVIRONMENT, CHANGE YOUR LIFE.

Just as a snake sheds its skin, we must shed our past over and over again.

BUDDHA

After the death of her husband, Jan started remodeling her kitchen. "Every time there was bad news on the variety of lawsuits I found myself in after my husband's death, I did something to the kitchen," she reports. "New cabinets one day, a new rug the next—you name it, I changed it up. I suppose the process gave me a creative outlet, but it also gave me something under my complete control when there was so much else that was out of my control. The remodeled kitchen made me feel good. It was light and cheery. And I needed light and cheery."

Jan's kitchen remodeling efforts reflect what Canadian businesswoman Emmanuelle Stathopoulous tells us about the power of environment. "Even small changes in our environment can result in substantial changes in our behavior," says Emmanuelle, "especially during times of crisis." This insight forms the heart of her business, Your Place and You (*www.yourplaceandyou.com*). Emmanuelle's background in environmental psychology combines with her eye for design to help people build personal sanctuaries that feed their souls.

Psychological Decluttering

"After the death of my first husband," Emmanuelle recalls, "I discovered the importance of a supportive home environment. I refer to the process as 'psychological decluttering.' It's all about connecting with your inner self and leaving behind what no longer serves you and keeps you stuck in repeated negative patterns of behavior. Decluttering of both the mind and space allows for a reduction of confusion, stress, and worry."

Emmanuelle reminds us that, when we experience loss through the death of a loved one, our minds and hearts are totally consumed with unbearable pain that is reflected everywhere around us. "We see it in photographs or a favorite armchair; we hear it in the music playing on the radio. We smell it in a woolen sweater that we don't dare wash so the person's scent will still be present in our home. These objects tell the story of our partnership and love.

"At first this is how it should be," says Emmanuelle. "You want to be surrounded by anything related to your beloved, anything that makes you feel their presence and reminds you of them. Their shoes in the hall that you don't dare put away mean the world to you when you come back home every day. You want to live in that shrine of a home comforted by all their personal objects.

"After several months, however, my soul began to feel exhausted by the constant and relentless pain of the familiar and I needed a change. This is when I decided to leave our tiny home and move back to our old house. It was my opportunity to turn what had been our house into one that would be exclusively mine. The sheer realization that I did not have to think of what he would have wanted, liked, or needed and that I had absolute freedom of choice felt both frightening and exhilarating. I was used to thinking for two.

"I could choose whatever furniture I wanted, and put it wherever I pleased without any constrictions or practical restrictions," Emmanuelle recalls. "I did not have to consider where I would fit all his electronic equipment or his collection of memorabilia. I had plenty of space to put whatever I liked, wherever I wanted. I was in total control."

It never occurred to Emmanuelle how much of her own wants and needs she had buried over all those years. She doesn't remember feeling constrained. "[But] all of a sudden, I was presented with a beautiful empty canvas on which to draw my new me, my new identity, myself without him. It was such an unknown and brand-new feeling, as I was used to thinking in terms of 'we' in everything. There were moments I missed the mess he usually left behind and the liveliness of a well-lived space. The emptiness and silence felt devastating but gradually turned into something creative.

"This whole process helped me birth the new me," she maintains. "I went from a helpless, traumatized, overwhelmed, utterly shattered, and desperate widow, to a courageous, self-confident, assertive, and capable woman. My warrior spirit! My deceased husband was still there, in photos, objects, and the wooden piano. Yet this was my space and my home now. He was still part of it, but not living in it anymore. And this is how it should be, as I was the one left behind to continue with my life alone without him."

Here are some tips from Emmanuelle's experience:

- ***Don't be too quick to give away the belongings of your loved one:*** At the early stages of grief, your desire to feel "normal" again and get rid of the unbearable pain may cloud your judgment and you may regret giving away certain things later. There is no rush; take your time. If you find yourself in a situation where you do need to rush, consider putting everything in boxes to sort at a later date.

- ***Postpone all major and critical decisions for at least a year, if possible:*** Don't sell the house and move to another continent three months after your loss! This is an attempt to escape grief and it doesn't usually work. Grief will catch up with you at a later moment once the excitement of the new environment wears off and you are left alone in your everyday reality.

- ***Meet your new reality with an open mind; leave your baggage behind:*** Five years after her husband's passing, at age fifty-three, Emmanuelle tells us, she moved to Canada to join her present partner. It wasn't easy, no matter the love and excitement of the new relationship and environment. Even though she was willingly, eagerly, and consciously moving on, she was still carrying her past with her. You must learn to leave your baggage behind.

46
JUST CLEAN SOMETHING.

I understand now, how grief strips you bare, shows you all of the things you don't want to know. There isn't a moment where you are done, when you can neatly put it away and be truly done.

ELIZABETH SCOTT, AMERICAN AUTHOR (1972–)

"Please can you just take care of my husband for a couple of days so that I can clean my house?" That is what Deborah asked the hospice nurse. "I got lost in scrubbing a bathroom floor or cleaning a window to see the reflection of the sun. Sweeping a floor with the vacuum cleaner and wiping down the cob webs in the corner of a room felt so good to me as I concentrated only on the doing and nothing else.

"It sounds really strange I know," Deborah says. "But what I didn't know at the time was that the simple act of cleaning, decluttering, or engaging in activities or tasks gives people a sense of control and a temporary escape from a painful reality." Retail therapy is another form of movement—shopping for things we probably don't need. But the action makes us feel good at the time. Retail therapy has served many of us well!

There is a good and bad side to movement, however. We can continue to fill our schedules, every waking hour, with "something" in order to cover the aspects of our lives that are difficult to deal with. Or we can engage in the distraction mindfully, knowing that it's a refresher, a short-term reprieve and not a solution. So on the days when you feel as if you just can't go on, cleaning, shopping, engaging in yoga, or filling your schedule so there are no free hours left can help. Just don't use movement consistently to mask your suffering or to avoid your reality.

WIT KIT TOOLS FOR CARRYING WHAT CANNOT BE FIXED

1. Do you have a support group? Are there people in your life who have gone through the same types of trials and tribulations? Write in your WIT Kit journal how it feels to connect with people who understand what you're experiencing. Identify two people with whom you have a lot in common. Reach out to these people and ask for their help.

2. Consider seeking a qualified therapist or grief coach. Ask your friends or doctor for referrals, or check online for a women's center in your area that has a list of reputable therapists.

3. How can you change up your environment as Emmanuelle did? Why not spend an afternoon with your journal in hand and magazines in the other. Tear out pages of homes and furnishings that call to you, or architecture that you love. Pinterest is also a great place for imagining your new environment. Make a Pinterest board and add to it as you see things that inspire you. Don't get caught up in what you can and cannot afford; just allow yourself to dream. You are in the planning phases for the environment you can build to support you in your next act.

CHAPTER EIGHT

FACING NAYSAYERS

*When you get into a tight place
and everything goes against you,
till it seems as though you could
not hang on a minute longer,
never give up. For that is just the
place and time that the tide will
turn.*

**HARRIET BEECHER STOWE,
ACTIVIST AND WRITER
(1811–1896)**

47
PERSIST.

If you have never been called a defiant, impossible woman . . . have faith there is yet time. For well-behaved women rarely make history.

ANITA BORG, COMPUTER SCIENTIST (1949–2003)

Being a Different Drummer

We four have pursued dreams and lives that were not ordinary for women of our backgrounds and cultures. There was nothing in our family histories that could ever have predicted that we would be successful in the endeavors we chose. But we were! We said earlier that the one commonality among the four of us was loss. There is a second— *tenacity*. There are very few things in life of which we are certain. One thing we do know, however, is that smart women persist even when success is elusive, failure has struck, and the road ahead seems unending.

On the path to achieving your dreams, expect to face naysayers. These non-believers are sometimes innocent, but they sometimes act with intent. Some deliberately do or say things to derail your dreams out of spite, while others supposedly do or say these things out of "love." We have all encountered them. Sometimes they are even the very people about whom we care most deeply—our mothers or daughters, our close friends or fathers, our spouses or colleagues. They may have told us what we could not do, be, say, think, or become. In most cases, they probably believed that they had our best interests at heart. And there may even have been a bit of truth in what they said. The trick is to learn to harvest the truth, extract the value, and let the rest go so you can pursue your dreams.

Some people, on the other hand, don't have your best interests at heart. They may work to thwart your dreams out of jealousy or . . . who knows what. We call these people "energy vampires."

"YOU CAN'T LEAVE, LAURA —
I'M MADLY IN NEED WITH YOU."

Energy Vampires

Have you ever left a meeting or a social function feeling mentally or physically exhausted without knowing why? Judith Orloff, physician and professor of clinical psychiatry at UCLA, coined the term "energy vampires" in her book *Positive Energy*. Energy vampires are "takers." They lie in wait, ready to suck up every last bit of precious energy you have. Dr. Orloff identified the different types of people lurking within your life and workplace who are just waiting to suck the life right out of you.

- *The Sob Sister*: She is always whining—the person with the "poor me" attitude. Offered solutions, she never stops complaining.

- *The Drama Queen*: She has flair, a real knack for taking everyday life and turning it into off-the-charts drama. To the drama queen, everything is a crisis.

- *The Blamer*: She has a sneaky way of making you feel guilty. She always has a negative comment to make about everything or everyone.

- **The Fixer-Upper**: She is desperate for you to fix her end-less problems. Her neediness lures you in until she has monopolized your time.

- **The Go-for-the-Jugular Friend**: She cuts you down with sarcastic comments. Her vindictiveness spares no room for your feelings.

During times of transition, we need to conserve all of our precious energy so we can be proactive rather than reactive. That means being on the alert for energy vampires who are trying to suck dry your enthusiasm, confidence, and vision. Review the list to see if any of these descriptions match people at work or at home who seem to be at their best when you're at your worst. Next time they start to denigrate you, interrupt them and say: "If you have a suggestion on how I can succeed at this, it's welcome. If not, please realize that you are not helping me—and keep your thoughts to yourself."

48
LISTEN TO YOUR BELIEFS, NOT YOUR DOUBTS.

I find that the very things that I get criticized for, which is usually being different and just doing my own thing and just being original, are the very things that make me successful.

SHANIA TWAIN, GRAMMY-WINNING SINGER (1965–)

The World Belongs to Dreamers

In looking back, Anne Robinson can understand how people thought she was marching to the beat of a very different drum. It was the height of the disco era, and John Travolta was center stage in *Saturday Night Fever*. But Anne believed in her heart that people would buy good piano music, even in the face of naysayers.

Anne signed George Winston to her new record label, called Windham Hill. Her business objective was to create a company that would touch the souls as well as the hearts of music lovers worldwide. "I traveled up and down the California coast," Anne told us, "in a dilapidated Volkswagen Beetle selling tapes of wondrous music. I attempted to build a community of music lovers by getting to know them and to understand their interests.

"Today, we call what I was doing 'one-to-one' marketing! My sophisticated customer database was an old shoebox with the name, address, and comments of most every person who had purchased a Windham Hill record." Anne built her love for good music into a multi-national company with just a dream, a shoebox full of names, and an unrelenting passion.

Imagine a world without Anne Robinson, Stevie Wonder, the Beatles, or Barbra Streisand—a world with no cell phones or tablet computers. If these individuals had listened to their naysayers, we would have missed out on all their talent, vision, and wisdom. Actress Jodie Foster said that, if she had listened to the naysayers of Hollywood, she never would have made a single movie. Debbi Fields founded a cookie empire by refusing to listen to those, including her husband, who thought selling cookies was a dumb idea! Naysayers have been present ever since Eve left the Garden of Eden. You've undoubtedly encountered some yourself. They say things like this:

- You need to be more realistic.

- Why can't you just be satisfied with what you have?

- You dreamer—always taking risks that never work out.

- Why can't you be more like your (brother, sister, friend)?

- If you don't watch out, this is going to backfire.

- Do you realize how much you have to lose if you do this?

- There you go again with your pie-in-the-sky ideas.

- You've always got your head in the clouds. What now?

- You're so selfish. You only think of what you want.

Since there seems to be no chance of naysayers becoming extinct, accept them for what they are and expect them to be an ever-present part of your life's journey. That said, be very clear that you will stop listening to them. Vow to start listening to your dreams, not their doubts. Seek out people who tell you how you can make your dream work.

49
TAKE BACK YOUR POWER.

The most common way people give up their power is by thinking they don't have any.

ALICE WALKER, WRITER (1944–)

Advocate for You

Michealene spent much of her life waiting for someone to notice her. She hoped that someone would come to her aid and give her the guidance and/or support she wanted and felt she deserved. She was disappointed. "I can't say I magically woke from a deep sleep and valued myself one day," says Michealene. "But after years of working hard and seeing the fruit of my labors go to other people, I realized I was the one who was giving away all of my power. I didn't have anyone to blame but myself. That was when I realized the only person who could rescue me was me."

To overcome the naysayers, you have to become your own advocate. And rest assured—not all naysayers are external. All too often, the biggest naysayer in a woman's life is herself. Do any of the phrases below sound familiar?

- Oh, I can't make a living at this!

- This wouldn't be a real job!

- How could anyone find me attractive?

- I wouldn't be a good mom.

- How dare I think I can do this?

- Oh, I actually love doing this, but . . .

- Who am I to think that I could go after this?

- I don't deserve this.

- Oh, my God, what am I doing taking this risk?

Fortunately, we all have the ability to overcome our tendency to be our own worst critics. Dr. Martin Seligman, the father of positive psychology, notes that many therapists are changing the nature of their work. Instead of delving into people's pasts and identifying what happened to them, they are now concentrating their efforts on helping clients take responsibility for making themselves more functional. He calls this "a sea change." Rather than focusing on what damages people, we should try to understand what makes them strong.

Do you have an inner judge who is quick to tell you how inadequate you are? Turn that critic into a coach. If that voice starts to tell you your dream is unrealistic and impossible, tell it the steps you're taking to make it possible. If this inner naysayer scoffs at your plans, remind it of Jodie Foster, Anne Robinson, and Debbi Fields. Then get up, get out, and make a difference in the world.

50
REFUSE TO BE IMPRISONED BY YOUR PAST.

I know God will not give me anything I can't handle. I just wish that He didn't trust me so much.

MOTHER TERESA, ALBANIAN-BORN CATHOLIC NUN AND ACTIVIST (1910–1997)

Resilience Is Something You Do

We live in California—a place people have been coming to for a couple of hundred years to leave their pasts behind and invent new futures. In a boom-and-bust cycle that began with the Gold Rush and continues today in the spirit of Silicon Valley, "California Dreaming" has taught us much about reinvention and the power of resiliency. And what Californians have known for years, scientists have just proven. Resiliency research conducted over the past decade has proven that all people have the capacity to overcome odds and bounce back.

Dr. Martin Seligman sheds more light on resiliency and how different people respond to adversity:

> On one end are people who fall apart into depression, and even suicide. In the middle are most people, who at first react with symptoms of depression and anxiety but within a month or so are, by physical and psychological measures, back where they were before the trauma. That is

THIS IS NOT THE LIFE I ORDERED

resilience. On the other end are people who show post-traumatic growth. They, too, first experience depression and anxiety, often exhibiting full-blown PTSD, but within a year they are better off than they were before the trauma. These are the people of whom Friedrich Nietzsche said, "That which does not kill us makes us stronger."

Dr. Seligman states that the single most important factor in resilience is being optimistic. The good news about optimism is that it is an emotion within our control. It's all about how we interpret events, ourselves, and outcomes. So resilience through optimism is something we can learn to do and to be.

Dr. Edith Grotberg of the University of Alabama, head of the International Resiliency Project, shared her research on why some people are able to bounce back and others aren't. Her findings include the following:

- There is no timeline, no set period, for finding the strength to overcome. Even one-third of poor, neglected, and abused children are capably building better lives by the time they are teenagers.

- Faith, be it in the future or in a higher power, is an essential ingredient in becoming resilient.

- Most resilient people don't go it alone. In fact, they don't even try. People who cope well with adversity are able to ask for help.

- Setting goals and planning for the future are strong factors in overcoming adversity and doubt. A belief in yourself and the ability to recognize your strengths is important.

Dr. Grotberg said their most important finding is that resilience is "something you do, not something you have." In other words, it's not a characteristic you're either blessed with or not. It's a skill you can develop.

"SWEETIE, SOMETHING'S COME UP. MIND RAISING THE KIDS?"

Esteem-able Acts

Spend some time with Francine Ward—a woman who changed from drug-addicted prostitute to Georgetown-educated lawyer—and you will immediately be drawn in by her resilience and her positive energy. She is brilliant, always impeccably dressed, and stylish. Yet, the Francine Ward of today is far from where she started.

As a young girl, Francine says, she got the message. Told repeatedly that she would not amount to anything, she believed that dreams were for girls who were rich, charmed, and white—not for girls like her. Francine took the message to heart and, by the age of fourteen, was strung out on heroin and well on her way to becoming an alcoholic. By eighteen, she was living as a homeless woman on the streets of New York. By twenty-one, she was supporting her drug and alcohol habits as a prostitute. At twenty-six, while walking drunk on the streets in Las Vegas, Francine was hit by a car and severely injured. She was told that she would never walk again. This time, Francine forgot to listen to the message.

Refusing to be imprisoned by the challenging circumstances of her present or her past, Francine not only learned to walk again, she also dramatically changed her life. "It was the end of my old life and the beginning of a life beyond my wildest imaginings," she relates. Today, Francine walks through life as a Georgetown University-educated lawyer, the owner of a successful business, the author of several best-selling books, and a loving wife.

Having traded the streets of New York for a home in the hills of Mill Valley, California, Francine attributes her transformation to something she calls "esteem-able acts." "These are the conscious, consistent daily actions a woman can take toward becoming the person she barely dreams she can be," says Francine.

Francine is the kind of woman you need to think about at two in the morning when you can't sleep because your life seems filled with insurmountable obstacles. She demonstrates that, by taking responsibility for her choices and her actions, any woman can call forth the remarkable resilience of the human spirit. We're blessed to know Francine, and you can be too. Her book *52 Weeks of Esteemable Acts: A Guide to Right Living* is a treasure chest of wisdom. You can also go to her website at *www.esteemableacts.com* for more information. It's a good place to visit on a sleepless night.

Stories like Francine's prove to us that resilience is an approach to life that you choose. Being resilient is a verb that is based on you acting on your own behalf. What is one thing you can do today so that you are not imprisoned by your situation?

WIT KIT TOOLS FOR FACING NAYSAYERS

1. In your WIT Kit journal, label the top of a page Naysayers in My Life. Thinking back to your childhood and working your way to the present time, write down the names of people who seemed to be more interested

in having you fail than succeed. And yes, this list may include you.

2. Go back over your list and write down anything you remember these people saying or doing to discourage you. Include the circumstances surrounding what happened and describe how their negative input affected you. Now, reject those naysayers—literally. Put a big X across each of their names. Tell yourself that you are going to take back your power and not let their attempts to undermine you continue. From now on, anytime you start to think of how someone tried to derail your dreams, picture yourself X-ing them out.

3. Label another page in your journal My Supporters. List the names of all the people who have supported you, encouraged you, believed in you, and told you that you could do it. Describe their positive impact and how their support has affected you. Now, circle those names. Put big stars by these individuals. From now on, seek out and honor these supporters (and yes, this includes yourself).

4. Make energy vampires and supporters the topic of a kitchen-table group. Suggest that everyone do this exercise, and then give each participant fifteen minutes to share her insights. How are you each going to honor the supporters in your lives? What are you going to say the next time someone tries to derail your dreams? How are you going to become coaches rather than critics of yourselves?

CHAPTER NINE

REBOUNDING FROM MISTAKES, MISERY, AND MAYHEM

*Great dreams . . . never even
get out of the box. It takes an
uncommon amount of guts to
put your dreams on the line, to
hold them up and say, "How good
or how bad am I?" That's where
courage comes in.*

**ERMA BOMBECK,
HUMORIST AND WRITER
(1927–1996)**

51
UNDERSTAND THAT SUCCESS OFTEN COMES DISGUISED AS A DUMB IDEA.

Have some fire in your belly. Become unstoppable. Be a force of nature. Be better than anyone who shows up. And don't give a damn what anyone thinks.

SHONDA RHIMES, AMERICAN TV PRODUCER (1970–)

Greatness Stems from Dumb and Weird

We've become convinced that success often comes disguised as a "dumb" idea—or at least as an idea that may seem "dumb" to others. Paul McCartney perhaps said it best: "It's not the people who are doing 'weird' things that are weird. It's the people who are calling people weird who are weird!" Bravo. We agree that pioneers and dreamers may be called "dumb" and "weird," but many of their inventions and creations have changed the world for the better.

In 1976, Anita Roddick's husband informed his wife and their two children that he had decided to fulfill a lifelong ambition—to ride a horse from Brazil to New York. He figured he would be gone for six to twelve months. Imagine his family's surprise! Faced with the dilemma of how to support herself and her two children while her husband rode into the sunset, Anita turned to what she knew best—concocting homemade cosmetics, lotions, and oils. Anita opened a tiny shop in the English resort town of Brighton, and the Body Shop was born. Today, there are Body Shops in forty-seven countries.

Kathleen Wentworth went to law school. She succeeded in her chosen path and was a successful prosecuting attorney who aggressively put murderers, pedophiles, and other unsavory characters behind bars. Yet what Kathleen really wanted to do was fly. She signed up for flying lessons and, after getting her pilot's certification, began to rack up the hundreds of hours needed to become a commercial pilot.

Today, Kathleen Wentworth is known as Captain Wentworth. She became the first woman captain for United Airlines.

Twins Jeanne and Jane Ford opened a small makeup store and focused on making problem-solving products that target particular beauty dilemmas. For instance, their top-selling product (over 10 million bottles sold) is Benetint, a rose-hued stain for lips and cheeks that was originally invented for an exotic dancer who wanted something to make her nipples appear pinker! Today, Benefit Cosmetics is nearing the billion-dollar mark in revenue and is known for its quirky packaging and whimsical attitude. Its company motto is: "Laughter is the best cosmetic . . . so grin and wear it."

Condi Rice grew up in the segregated streets of Alabama where her father told her: "Even if you can't order a hamburger and be served at Woolworth's, that doesn't mean you can't grow up and become the president of the United States." Condi served as the first black woman Secretary of State.

Rose Guilbault was the child of Hispanic migrant workers who made their living picking fruits and vegetables in the California fields. Rose became the first female in her family to attend college and the first Hispanic female TV producer and host.

Mimi Silbert took a thousand dollars, a bunch of Christmas trees, and twenty ex-convicts to begin an experiment that grew into Delancey Street—one of the most successful rehabilitation programs in the world. Running for-profit operations staffed by ex-convicts and former drug addicts, Mimi and her staff are the successful owners of a restaurant, a bookstore, a construction company, a moving company, and, yes, still the best damned Christmas-tree lot in San Francisco.

Kristi Yamaguchi was born with deformed feet. For the first two years of her life, she wore plaster casts and foot braces. As therapy for her feet, her parents enrolled her in dance lessons. But it was ice-skating that captured her heart. As a youngster, she woke up at four every morning to practice on the ice for five hours before heading to school. Ironically, when she was selected to represent the United States at the 1992 Winter Olympics, she was considered the underdog. Kristi won a gold medal.

When these women were devising their dreams, they were often told that their plans were "dumb." But the dreams they had the courage to follow and realize have made a positive difference in the world—and in their own lives. Do you have a dream that others think is dumb? Have you considered that perhaps your idea may just be ahead of its time? Are people telling you it's crazy just because it's not already common? Maybe you are a pioneer who is daring to be the first at something instead of blending in with the pack. Seek out fellow inventors or creative types who will support your innovation instead of sabotaging it.

52
SEEK OUT A DREAM CATCHER.

Dreams are illustrations from the book your soul is writing about you.

MARSHA NORMAN, PLAYWRIGHT (1947–)

Dream Big

A "dream catcher" is someone who encourages innovation and creativity and supports people in the realization of their dreams. Many years ago, we learned about a dream catcher named Dr. Ivan Scheier. During his long career, Dr. Scheier helped hundreds of nonprofit organizations and communities achieve their dreams. At the age of seventy-eight, he created Voluntas, a residential retreat aimed at stimulating creative, expansive, and practical dreaming about communities and volunteerism.

"A world in which people have no chance of achieving their dreams is not, to me, a world in which I would choose to live," says Scheier. In his role as dream catcher, Scheier listened to hundreds of people with ideas, hopes, and inspirations who lacked the financial resources to bring their dreams to life. He developed some rules for dreamers that smart women can use in making their dreams come true:

1. ***Realize that nothing happens right away.*** Stay with your dream and live close to your beliefs.

2. ***Dreams usually don't come about in the way you first visualize them.*** Don't expect them to. Be open to new opportunities and ideas. Reality is too complicated, and surprise is half the fun!

3. ***The only constants are your values.*** Keep compromise to a minimum on these, even when it comes disguised in nice names like team-building, negotiation, or consensus.

4. ***Seek cooperators in your dream.*** Dreams rarely survive their origins without evolution to a broader ownership. Get your ideas out in the universe and see whom they inspire.

5. ***Be flexible and uncompromising.*** Be as flexible about the implementation of your dream as you are uncompromising on the values of your vision. Avoid tight planning, and don't let your plan become an end in itself.

6. ***Money is never the main ingredient of dream achievement.*** Free yourself from major money needs insofar as it is reasonable and possible. The "if only I had the money" mind-set can result in neglect of other potentially more feasible approaches.

7. ***Look backward, not forward.*** When you get the blues—and dreamers do—don't look forward; look backward. Looking backward reminds you how many dreams have actually come true in your life, while looking forward only reminds you of the obstacles you face.

The Power of Dreaming

Ola Kizer wanted a college degree and, at the age of eighty-six, she finally got one by becoming the oldest undergraduate in more than 200 years at the University of Tennessee. Vowing never to return to the poverty she had known as a child, she figured the college degree would help her. "You have to hold onto your dreams," Kizer said. "It is not going to be easy. If you are rowing, you couldn't cross the ocean in one day. So stick with it and keep going." Kizer knows the power behind dreaming.

"OKAY, SAY WE SETTLE DOWN AND HAVE A NICE LIFE TOGETHER. WHAT'S IN IT FOR ME?"

Your dreams may not be as large and encompassing as Indira Gandhi's to save her native country of India or as courageous as Amelia Earhart's to take to the skies. You may or may not set your sights on inventing the next best-selling product or book, but your dream and your visions for your life are just as important. In fact, they are vitally important to your health and well-being.

Review Ivan Scheier's seven suggestions. Pick one that is particularly timely or relevant for you and discuss it at your kitchen-table group. Perhaps it is number seven—the counter-intuitive idea that it is best to look backward rather than forward. Reviewing your history and tapping into your successes may be just what you need to help you forge ahead with determination.

53
SCHEDULE A PAINT DATE.

Life is what we make it—always has been and always will be.

GRANDMA MOSES, PAINTER (1860–1961)

Garage Artists

"My introduction to the wisdom of women and its importance in rebuilding dreams began with a woman in my neighborhood who invited me to paint with her in her garage," Deborah recalls. "She insisted that I was an artist, even though I told her that my best attempt in art was a project in fifth grade consisting of glue, some crayons, and Popsicle sticks. She continued to badger me until I agreed to visit her garage and paint, if only to get her to quit pestering me!

"The 'paint date' rolled around, and I reluctantly appeared. Her two-car garage had been transformed into a wonderfully decorated and inviting art studio. The studio was overflowing with members of a local Presbyterian women's group, who ranged in age from twenty-five to eighty-six. Over coffee, tea, and fresh fruit, we painted on canvas and talked for nearly three hours. In those three hours, the women brought more collective wisdom into my life than I had encountered in three years. Although I am neither a Presbyterian nor an artist, it didn't matter. What mattered was that I was a woman in their community who needed to be supported through a transition."

Wisdom for Breakfast

Instead of painting to find a path to her dreams, Jan went to breakfast—a breakfast that would give her a whole new outlook on life. "I was feeling low," she says. "Depressed might be another word for it. I no longer had the best television job in the world, and my husband had recently died. I was putting on lipstick in the morning, kissing my kids, dealing with lawsuits, and I felt completely lost. I needed a job; I needed to support my kids. Truthfully, what I needed was to find myself again.

"One of my best friends, Debbi Fields (founder of Mrs. Fields Cookies) was coming to visit. I used Debbi as the perfect excuse to gather some incredible women for a breakfast I knew would be uplifting. Gathered round that morning were Debbi Fields, Jackie Speier, Nancy Olsen, Linda Howell, Anne Robinson, and Susie Tompkins. We shared fears, concerns, self-doubt, and lots of laughter.

"Debbi told us what it was like to be newly divorced after twenty years of marriage and five children. Debbi went on to remarry. She and her new husband, Mike Rose, were together for nineteen years before he died last year at age seventy-five. Her third daughter, Jennifer, just made her a grandmother for the second time. Debbi lives up to the title Glam-mother.

"Jackie spoke of learning to date after the death of her husband and running for the State Senate. Today, she is remarried and is the Congresswoman from San Francisco.

"Nancy talked of growing her company from one store to 126 nationwide, bringing in venture capital and subsequently being fired with no severance, no golden parachute, nothing. Today, Nancy is a high school counselor, having returned to her first love of teaching. She also plays percussion in a local concert band.

"Anne told us that this was the first day she was 'unemployed.' She had sold her company, and the new owners were exercising their option to remove her from the helm four years earlier than originally agreed. Anne has since formed a textile company and a music company, and she swims every day.

"Susie told us how she had survived the public disintegration of her marriage and the story behind her company, Esprit. Today, Susie is married to her high school sweetheart, Mark Buell, and they are living happily ever after.

"I remember feeling such an enormous amount of respect for each of these women. I also remember how good

I felt—how empowered. It was a feeling that lasted for a long time afterward. That breakfast gathering helped me realize I was not alone. We were all women in transition. A few days later, Jackie decided that our breakfast conversation should go on. She wanted us to join her at the Professional and Business Women's Conference and thought our 'breakfast topic' would be a great seminar. And this was the beginning of our kitchen-table group of friends."

54
FIND THREE WISE WOMEN.

Look at everything as though you were seeing it either for the first or last time.

BETTY SMITH, WRITER (1896–1972)

If you ever feel as if your shoulders are scraping the cement sidewalk, remember what Deborah found in the garage and Jan discovered over breakfast: Women have a remarkable way of helping other women. The wisdom of women can be a life raft when you are engulfed in a transition.

Wisdom is not something we are born with. It is the cumulative result of life lessons gained through personal experience. The good news is that we can "borrow" wisdom from other people. By accessing people who have "been there, done that," we can capitalize on their successes and avoid their errors.

The best news is that collective wisdom is available to every woman, no matter her community, background, or education. All she has to do is reach out to those around her who are willing to share and who have some of the characteristics that iconic psychologist Abraham Maslow identified as being "wise."

Maslow said wise people see things clearly and act in effective ways. They handle whatever arises in their lives with peace of mind and with effective and compassionate responses. They control important emotions like fear, anger, jealousy, hatred, and greed, because they know these emotions are the cause of human suffering. Wise people have strong ethical boundaries. They live compassionately, take full responsibility for their choices, and work to maintain a positive outlook on life—no matter the circumstances.

Finding Wisdom

We've come to believe that we each need at least three wise women in our lives. These mentors share how they have faced and overcome difficulties, and advise us on how we can do the same. By "going before us," they have learned what works and what doesn't. We no longer have to re-create the wheel, because we have the benefit of their experiences and support.

You may be thinking: "I agree, but where do I find one wise woman, let alone three?" Trust us when we say that wise women are everywhere. They can be found among your family members, in your workplace, in organizations and churches, and certainly in every community around the world. All you have to do is reach out to those around you who are willing to share their insights and observations.

Start by looking around and asking yourself: Whom do I admire? Whom do I respect for what she has accomplished or overcome? Who has been down the path I'm about to travel?

You may be thinking: "This person is busy. Why would she want to help me?" Good question. She'll want to help you if you honor the Three As of being a protégé: Ask. Act. Appreciate.

When you approach your proposed mentor, make sure your first words are: "I know you are busy, but may I have five minutes of your time?" This is a gracious way to let the woman know you're considerate of her other demands.

Next, describe your dilemma or your goal: I'm about to have my first child. Or I'm interested in launching my own business. Then ask if she is willing to share her own experience—perhaps a couple of things she wishes someone had told her when she was starting out. Take notes so she realizes how much you honor her input.

Be sure to thank your wise woman immediately and tell her how you intend to act on her suggestions. Then get back in touch to let her know how her advice worked out and how much you appreciate her contribution. If you ask, act, and appreciate, you make this a win-win situation for you and for the woman who has generously shared her wisdom.

WIT KIT TOOLS FOR REBOUNDING FROM MISTAKES, MISERY, AND MAYHEM

1. In your Wit Kit journal, make an entry of three big dreams you have—don't edit or critique them, just write them down. What aspect of your dreams can you build into your future right now? If you hope to write a book, can you simply begin to write a paragraph each day? If you want to launch a business, reach out to another business owner and get advice. Attend a trade show or call the SCORE group—a volunteer group of seasoned executives who advise small business owners.

2. Identify a "dream catcher" in your life, someone who inspires you to follow your dreams. The blue-haired lady was Deborah's. Start looking for your own special dream catcher.

3. In your Wit Kit journal, make a list of the wisest women you know. Some you may know personally, others may be famous women you cull from the rich history of our world. What do you admire about these women? What are their qualities? When you think of them, how do you feel? What can you learn from them?

CHAPTER 10

DESIGNING YOUR LIFE

*One of the most calming and
powerful actions you can take to
intervene in a stormy world is to
stand up and show your soul.*

**CLARISSA PINKOLA ESTES,
AMERICAN AUTHOR (1945–)**

55
DISRUPT YOURSELF.

In your life you are the greatest project you will ever get to work on. Create magic.

ELIZABETH GILBERT, AMERICAN AUTHOR (1969–)

Never Waste a Good Crisis

Industries and markets undergo disruption routinely. Take, for example, the hotel industry and Airbnb. The industry was turned upside down by Airbnb and forced to change in order to survive. This disruption theory was at work as well when computers changed the way we communicate and thereby changed our world. And the same forces of disruption and chaos in your own life can change the status quo in good ways.

Whitney Johnson had no business credentials, connections, or confidence when she started as a secretary to a retail sales broker at Smith Barney in midtown Manhattan. "It was the era of *Liars' Poker* and *Bonfire of the Vanities*," says Whitney, "and working on Wall Street was exciting. I started taking business courses at night and I had a boss who believed in me, which allowed me to bridge from secretary to investment banker. This rarely happens."

Soon, experts began to seek out Whitney's financial modeling and one of the world's richest men, Carlos Slim, even quoted her research. Clayton Christensen, a leading expert on innovation, recruited Whitney to become a cofounder of his investment fund. Working with Christensen led Whitney to apply what she had learned about disruption, chaos, and innovation in markets to people's lives and careers.

Whitney believes that people should purposely learn to "disrupt themselves" in an effort to be competitive in today's world. She makes the case that we can and should rethink the fundamentals of our lives, but we rarely do until crisis forces us to do so.

Chances are the crisis you find yourself in doesn't appear to be valuable. Trust us, it is. Challenges, uncomfortable as they may be, also afford us an incredible opportunity for learning. Whitney says that what we learn during times of disruption can often become the "superpowers" that will take us where we want to go next.

56
THINK LIKE AN ENGINEER.

My life didn't please me, so I created my life.

COCO CHANEL, FRENCH DESIGNER (1883–1971)

The Ten-Year Itch

Engineers are trained to see a structure where nothing exists. They create by designing under great constraints, as they have to use forces they can't change—like gravity. They also can't wait for every aspect of their undertaking to be understood or explained fully, so they learn to produce results under given conditions. They understand trade-offs and take the right risks. Val Grubb is an engineer by training who spent a decade in her chosen career—until a familiar thing entered her life. She calls it her "ten-year itch."

"I was about to get a big promotion," said Val, "and it required that I move to England. I turned the promotion down, quit my job, and moved to Los Angeles instead. I just knew something needed to change in my life and so I listened to that inner voice. I had saved up enough money to live for eight months without a job and I hit the ground running, determined to break into the close-knit cadre of influentials that work in entertainment. I've learned that, once I make a decision, I embrace it with gusto. I don't spend time in self-doubt. I ended up working for Barry Diller for two years and then I moved to New York City to help build Oxygen Media. I worked with incredible women like Gerry Laybourne and Oprah Winfrey. Life was great and I loved

Manhattan. Several years passed by. Then, before you know it, there it was—that ten-year itch was revisiting me.

"I really wanted to own my own company; I wanted to run my own show," says Val. "So while I was still at Oxygen Media, I started a business. That business contained all of the things I loved about my work and I designed it that way. Yet something was missing. I had lived in New York for eighteen years, but my heart was in New Orleans. So I devised a plan and strategy for moving to the Big Easy. I completed spreadsheets filled with information, calculated the risks, the upside, the downside, and came to the conclusion that it was the right decision.

"I moved to this wonderful city and I love it. I have become deeply involved in the community, participate in the Mardi Gras parade, and am now the President of the New Orleans Film Society. I always encourage people to engineer a life that contains all of the things you love. Use your imagination and then devise ways to achieve what you've planned."

57
BE CURIOUS.

Curiosity only does one thing, and that is to give. And what it gives you are clues on the incredible scavenger hunt of your life.

ELIZABETH GILBERT, AMERICAN AUTHOR (1969–)

We were introduced to a legendary course taught at Stanford University Design School aptly titled Designing Your Life. Bill Burnett, Executive Director of Stanford's design program, had previously worked developing and designing for the *Star Wars* franchise. He teamed up with Dave Evans, who led the design of Apple's first mouse and co-founded Electronic Arts. They then took their training as designer and engineer and applied the tools and mind-sets from their previous careers to designing people's lives. The course caught on like wildfire and, for many, it was life-changing. The great news is that now anyone can take the course online by signing up at Creative Live. In addition, Burnett and Evans have written a highly acclaimed book called *Designing Your Life: How to Build a Well-Lived, Joyful Life.*

"Designers," says Burnett, "don't think their way forward; they build their way forward." Burnett and Evans counsel that we need to "try stuff," because the more we try, the more we create a bias for action from within. "Life design," Burnett says, "is a journey. The more we can focus on the process and see what happens, the better lives we create for ourselves."

Curiosity is integral to design thinking. It's both a behavior and an emotion that fuels all of human development. We begin with a problem to solve or a dream we want to bring into reality. Curiosity can be a powerful agent that can help us figure out problems and build new realities. Yet often during such times, when we most need our natural curiosity, our fears can rise up and kill it. Fear shuts us down, while curiosity energizes us and expands our thinking of what is possible.

Earlier, we introduced you to Sara Little Turnbull. When Sara developed Corning Ware, the concept began with her curiosity. She wondered if the material that was used on space shuttles could be used in other ways. She noticed trends in the 1950s that demonstrated an interest in cooking and baking. Being curious helped her make the link between the aerospace material and the development of cookware.

While life is certainly not cookware, the same approach Sara used can be applied to life. You can imagine new beginnings, or a new career for yourself. Being curious about patterns—about your likes and dislikes, and about what brings you joy—are important factors. Your natural curiosity about these factors can help you figure out a path forward.

WIT KIT TOOLS FOR DESIGNING YOUR LIFE

1. Take out your journal and write up to two pages on where you want to be one year, three years, and five years from now. Put as much detail as possible in this assignment. Describe your environment, your clothes, your friends, and even the kinds of pets you will have. Reflect on what you have written. Do you see any patterns emerging? Write them down.

2. In your journal, draw a line down the middle of a blank page. On the left side of the page, write down your values. Values are character traits and people or things that you simply must have in your life. Come up with at least ten. Now narrow the ten down to five. You've just designed an important component of your life: the five values you must have in any endeavor. Now, on the right side of the page, write and describe how often in a day or a week you live your values. How can you make the necessary changes?

3. What did you dream about when you were a child? What did you wish to do or to be? If you dreamed of being an astronaut and that is not a goal for you today, is there some way you can incorporate the heavens and stars into your life right now? If you dreamed of being a famous singer, can you take a music lesson? Try to think of other things you may want to incorporate into your life design.

CHAPTER ELEVEN

LIGHT A CANDLE IN THE DARK

Every day you dare to dream, you fight back the darkness and add more light to the world.

**HOLLEY GERTH,
AMERICAN AUTHOR**

58
SHINE A LIGHT, DON'T CURSE THE DARK.

If you ask me what I came into this world to do, I will tell you: I came to live my life out loud.

EMILE ZOLA, FRENCH NOVELIST AND CRITIC (1840–1902)

Fire and Spark

Three words—*You will survive*—written by former Buddhist monk and best-selling author Jack Kornfield gave us hope during dark times. Dr. Kornfield states that we are never alone no matter our circumstances, because thousands of generations before us were survivors. They carried the lamp of humanity through difficult times and passed it on from one generation to the next. He points out that the same spirit that carried Nelson Mandela through years of imprisonment or survivors of the Holocaust through years of torture resides within each of us.

Extraordinary human beings shine a light in the darkness. Their stories help us realize that we were designed for all of the ups and downs that life holds for us. Their fire can tap a spark within us. Paola Gianturco is one such extraordinary woman who is helping to illuminate a dark world.

Paola Gianturco was among the first female executives at advertising firm Saatchi and Saatchi. She also co-developed the Executive Institutes on Women and Leadership at Stanford University, where Michealene met her when she participated in her course. After thirty-five years in corporate America, Paola decided to take a year off and focus only on what she loved—photography and travel. She wanted to learn about women in the developing world. Paola says she had no idea that she would begin a second career at the age of fifty-five by becoming an internationally acclaimed photojournalist and author. Today, at age seventy-eight, she has written many best-selling and award-winning books, among them *Women Who Light the Dark, Wonder Girls Changing Our World,* and *Grandmother Power—A Global Phenomenon.*

Frequent Flyer

Paola launched a new chapter in her life with the 3 million frequent flyer miles she and her husband had accumulated in the course of their careers. Those miles fueled her travels and assisted her in introducing the world to women and girls who are changing the future for their families. Paola reminds us that these women and girls are among the most vulnerable and the least literate and yet they have imagination and determination that lights the darkness in the midst of intractable problems.

In Africa, Paola documented the work of women and girls in rural Kenya, where there is no national water infrastructure. Young girls often walk seven hours each day to find water and bring it back for their families. Paola talks about Norma Audion Bois, who had searched for water for most of her life. She decided to start an NGO that now includes forty-three local women's groups whose work it is to get wells dug in schoolyards. Children can now wash their hands, preventing deadly disease, and girls are in school instead of searching for water.

In Senegal, Paola met grandmothers who were horrified that their daughters were dying in childbirth as a result of hemorrhaging from female genital mutilation. The grandmothers were determined to stop this practice, but it wasn't easy. Over a three-year period spent meeting with elders, religious figures, and community leaders, the grandmothers began conversations about good traditional practices that should be sustained. They also asked that everyone think about bad traditions that should be changed or abolished. Through wise conversations, the grandmothers gently persuaded over twenty villages to abandon female genital mutilation and child marriage.

No Emotion Is Ever Final

Paola is still traveling and photographing women from all over the world. She catches them in the acts of enhancing education, health, equality, and the environment. They are stopping child marriage, domestic violence, human trafficking, and war. She points to a hand-painted mural on her office wall that reads: No emotion is ever final. "I've discovered that women can always find a way to use their pain, their suffering, and their losses to channel it all into ways that help the world move forward," she explains. "When you meet a grandmother in an African village who is caring for her twelve AIDS-infected grandchildren because all five of her children have died from the disease, it's difficult to wallow in your own misery. There are women and young girls all over the world with very few resources or support who are doing miraculous work. Their courage is always contagious."

59
LEARN TO FORGIVE.

A strong woman loves, forgives, walks away, lets go, tries again and perseveres . . . no matter what life throws at her.

BEYONCÉ, AMERICAN MUSICIAN (1981–)

Betrayal Stings

Is it possible to forgive the hurtful aspects of betrayal that all too often impact women? It's not only possible; the act of forgiveness improves our health and well-being. Researchers at Johns Hopkins Medical Center say the act of forgiveness can reap huge rewards for your health, lowering the risk of heart attack, improving cholesterol levels and sleep patterns, and reducing pain, blood pressure, and levels of anxiety, depression, and stress.

Forgiveness, the researchers say, is not just about saying the words "I forgive." Rather it is an active process in which you make a conscious decision to let go of negative feelings *whether the object of your forgiveness deserves it or not.* This is the difficult lesson that Jan learned as she struggled to recover from her husband's betrayal.

"Betrayal. Where do I begin?" asks Jan. "Of course, I never thought he would cheat on me. That only happens to *other* women. One friend who had been married for thirty-nine years found out when she got a text message from her husband who was working in another city. In his text, he hoped she had gotten home safely and told her that he missed her. She thought it was odd, since she *was* at home. Soon another text arrived. It said he loved her and couldn't wait to see her again. Then she got it. Another friend told me how she checked the messages on their home answering service only to find her husband talking to another woman, completely unaware that their conversation was being recorded! When she confronted him about the other woman—he denied it. She held up the phone as proof.

"For me," Jan remembers, "I got an email addressed to Janet. Because my name also begins with a 'J,' I think that, in haste, he simply hit that send button and the email came to me. He told Janet that his marriage was over and that he wanted to see her again. When I read the email, I think all the blood rushed out of my body. I could feel my face get red-hot, yet the rest of me felt ice-cold. I knew our marriage was going through a rough spot. Looking back, I should have been wiser to all the signs."

Jan recalls that her first instinct was to do what she thought she should do—save the marriage. "I agreed to marriage counseling. The psychologist said he had seen many marriages go through one spouse cheating and yet the couple came back together and remained strong. We went through four months of counseling, together and separately. It was a waste of money and my time.

"During those four months, I was a wreck. The depth of hurt felt as if there was no bottom. I was crushed and mangled; I lost every bit of self-esteem I had ever had. I questioned whether I was a good wife. What did I do wrong? What can I do to make this work?

"Jackie looked at me and told me I was acting like an abused woman. I was so taken aback by her words that I replied in utter self-defense: 'Me? No, I'm not!' Of course, I was. To be clear, there was never any physical abuse, but emotional and verbal abuse, yes.

"It's been ten years since I got my final divorce papers. Some days, the sting of betrayal rears its ugly head. Some days, I can dismiss it. One day, I hope it won't matter."

Forgiveness Heals

Eva Mozes Kor has been making the conscious decision to forgive for over half a century. When we first met Eva, we were struck by how small and fragile she appeared. When she spoke, however, all that frailty disappeared. Eva is a survivor of the Holocaust who emerged from a trauma-filled childhood to become the embodiment of the human spirit's ability to overcome and forgive.

Growing up in the only Jewish family in a small Romanian town, Eva was sent to Auschwitz as a ten-year-old child. She and her twin sister, Miriam, were separated from the rest of their family and became part of a group of thirteen pairs of twins who were subjected to experiments by Josef Mengele during World War II.

"Living in Auschwitz was a full-time job," Eva observes. "Dying was very easy. In order to survive Auschwitz, in my opinion, people needed two things: a lot of luck, and an unbelievable will to live. If you didn't have both, you would die."

In an act that is symbolic, Eva returns to Auschwitz every summer to host tours for those interested in educating themselves about the Holocaust. On every tour, she reads aloud letters of forgiveness to her tormentors.

"I discovered that I had the power to forgive," she explains. "No one could give me that power, and no one could take it away. And it made me feel unbelievably good that I, the little victim, even had the power to forgive the angel of death of Auschwitz." For Eva, anger is a "seed for war," while forgiveness is a "seed for peace." She firmly believes in the power of forgiveness to heal wounds. She advises us all to forgive even our worst enemies, because it heals us.

"For any person who has been hurt by anybody," Eva maintains, "be the hurt big or very small—they don't have to carry that hurt. They have the power. No one can give them that power. They have the power to heal themselves. If they realize they have the power, try it and see what happens. It costs zero. It's not a very expensive thing to do."

From Victim to Leader

Earlier Michealene introduced us to Betty Makoni, yet our book would not be complete if we didn't tell more of Betty's story, as she is truly a woman who lights up a dark sky. Makoni grew up in Zimbabwe where she has worked most her life to protect her country's young girls from sexual abuse. In Zimbabwe, where the HIV virus is rampant, men with the virus believe that sexual relations with a virgin will cure the disease. This myth has resulted in some of the worst cases of sexual abuse in the world. "The youngest girl I ever came across was a day-old baby who was raped," said Betty. Through her Girl Child Network she has helped rescue 35,000 girls from abuse.

Raped at age 6, Betty said her mother wouldn't allow her to report it. "She said, 'Shh, we don't say that in public,'" Betty remembers. Three years later she witnessed her father murder her mother. In that moment, Betty said she realized the potentially deadly consequence of a woman's silence.

Betty procured a piece of land and opened the organization's first empowerment village, designed to provide a haven for girls who have been abused. Girls are either rescued or referred to the village by social services, the police, and the community. The healing begins as soon as a girl arrives.

"In the first seventy-two hours, a girl is provided with emergency medication, reinstatement in school, as well as counseling," Betty told us. It is important to her that the girls are in charge of their own healing. "It gives them the confidence to transform from victims to leaders," she explained.

But for Betty, taking action came with a high personal cost. She was forced to flee her native country. Betty said: "I left Zimbabwe because my life was in danger as a result of my project being interpreted politically." Today, she lives with her family in the United Kingdom and her work in Zimbabwe shows no signs of slowing down.

60
APPLY THESE LESSONS LEARNED.

Life should not be a journey to the grave with the intention of arriving safely in an attractive and well-preserved body, but rather to skid sideways, chocolate in one hand, martini in the other, body thoroughly used up, totally worn out, and screaming, "Woo hoo—what a ride!"

ANONYMOUS

Wiser and Richer

In looking back over our many years of friendship, we realize that the "lives we didn't order" were molded and melded and reinvented into lives we treasure. At times, we would willingly have traded them for what was behind Door Number Three. Yet, we are wiser because of our life experiences and we are richer. Richer in ways that money can never buy—in spirit, in wisdom, and in joy.

Here, we have shared sixty ways that we've found to help us get through, around, over, or under what life handed us. We hope you have enjoyed these stories and learned from our lessons. More important, we hope you are motivated to follow up and apply these lessons in your everyday life. Please contact us with your insights via our website *www.kitchentablefriends.com*. We also love to hear your stories. Until then, best wishes in your endeavor to turn lives you may not have ordered into ones you love immensely.

WIT KIT TOOLS FOR LIGHTING A CANDLE IN THE DARK

1. Pull out your journal and write an entire page naming the things in your life that are good and right. This exercise helps you remember your ability to rise above what confronts you.

2. Volunteer with an organization that is addressing an issue in your community. Mentor a young girl. By volunteering and mentoring, you take your mind away from your own problems and gain a sense of accomplishment. Who knows whom you may meet and where it may lead? You'll be giving a part of yourself in a meaningful way. It will feel good.

3. Employ the "weather practice." Think of your thoughts and emotions as passing weather. Like storm clouds, they will pass, and the sun will rise and shine tomorrow. Remember what Paola Gianturco said: No emotion is ever final.

EPILOGUE

We treasure feedback from our readers. Here's how several have applied the lessons from this book in their own lives.

DON'T REINVENT THE WHEEL

"I just finished your book. It has motivated me to keep going. I am in a transitional phase in my life right now. My husband passed away almost three and a half years ago from metastatic melanoma. He battled for seven and a half years. I was a caregiver for those seven and a half years, so I was pretty lost. Sometimes I forget how far I've come and how much I've learned, and your book helped me to remember. As you state, we can be our own worst critics and not believe in ourselves as much as we should. It is exciting when I read similar stories and realize that I don't have to reinvent the wheel to get through this. Thanks for writing a book for 'like-minded' women."

MAKE A COMEBACK

"I picked up your book purely by accident and it has become an inspiration. Ten years ago, I divorced and it was crushing. He was the light of my life; he had an affair and left me for her. My company let me go because they were selling the operation. I was absolutely crushed. I had totally lost confidence in the strong, independent woman that I was and became the old granny I vowed I would never be.

Then I read your book. Everything you said was so re-affirming and so full of compassion. As I read, I stopped feeling sorry for myself—I mean, it's not as if I had ever lain on a tarmac full of bullets bleeding to death! I forced myself to go back to working out, started contacting people again, and reached out to those close to me for help. I no longer look down when people ask what I am doing; I quickly tell them I took some time off to relax and am now actively looking for work. I have joined Rotary again, am volunteering for a couple of organizations to make contacts, and am lunching myself into another weight gain I am sure!

I wanted you wonderful ladies to know how much you helped. I consider you four on my list of supporters! Thank you for helping me come back."

WORK AT IT

"Today is my wedding anniversary—thirty-seven years. I am in Santa Fe and my husband is in Wisconsin. The way it worked out, no biggie. I am sixty-four and wondering where I am going from here. By the time I finished your book, I knew what I needed and wanted to do. I came to the realization that I have a lot of time to implement my dreams and how to go about it. As I was putting my things away in the guest house/office of the owner of the beautiful ranch where my son is house-sitting, I realized I was working at the desk of a multi-millionaire, and it felt right."

FIND THE UNEXPECTED JOY

"I have been widowed for four years and I found your book inspiring, full of great ideas. And I know it applies to just about every woman in my life! I know women will be as inspired as I was. I look for every opportunity that might give a glimmer of hope that there is life after death. Your book does that."

REFERENCES

5. LEARN THE SECRETS OF THE BLUE-HAIRED LADY.

PBWC (*www.pbwc.org*), founded by Jackie Speier, is the largest women's conference in the West.

Indiana Conference for Women (*indianaconferencefor-women.com*) founded by Deborah C. Stephens and Billie Dragoo is the largest women's conference in the Midwest.

8. BE WILLING TO MAKE GREAT MISTAKES.

"The Oops Center," *Exploration Research Journal*. Press Release, Vanderbilt University, December 14, 2000.

Dr. Bjorn Olsen, Harvard University, founder of *Journal of Negative Results*. CBS Radio Interview with Charles Osgood, May 4, 2004.

12. DON'T WAIT UNTIL YOU ARE DEPRESSED OR DESPERATE (OR BOTH) TO NETWORK.

UCLA press release summary and findings of *UCLA Landmark Study on Friendship*, featuring Laura Cousins Klein, PhD, June 2003.

Nurses Health Studies, Harvard, Chan School of Public Health, November, 2012.

14. MOVE ON, MOVE UP, OR MOVE OUT.

Russ Harris, *The Reality Slap* (New York: New Harbinger Publications, 2012), p. 2.

17. REALIZE THAT RISKS ARE PART OF THE PACKAGE.

Gail Sheehy in conversation at Indiana Conference for Women, November 2014, and from her book, *Daring* (New York: William Morrow, 2014).

Laura Lisawood, excerpt from Women's Leadership Project, Kennedy School of Government, Harvard University, June 1996.

21. WALK THROUGH FIELDS OF FEAR.

From Vornida Seng and excerpts from her interview with *People Magazine*, May 2001.

25. WEAR A COURAGE BRACELET.

Mary Anne Radmacher, *Lean Forward into Your Life* (San Francisco: Conari Press, 2005), p. 4.

26. KNOW THAT COURAGE ISN'T ONLY OWNED BY HEROES.

Marianne Williamson, *A Return to Love: Reflections on the Principles of a Course in Miracles* (New York: Harper Collins, 1996), p. 190.

In conversation with Anucha Brown Sanders at Indiana Conference for Women, 2016.

27. WHEN YOU ARE SHORT ON DOLLARS, BE RICH IN SPIRIT.

National Center for Women and Aging, "Sitting Pretty or Sitting Duck," 1998 Findings.

29. DON'T WAIT UNTIL YOUR FINANCIAL DNA IS ON LIFE SUPPORT.

In consultation and in conversation and with thanks to Lori Sackler, author of *The M Word: The Money Talk Every Family Needs to Have About Wealth and Their Financial Future* (New York: McGraw Hill, 2013), and *The M Word: The Money Talk Every Family Needs to Have About Wealth and Their Financial Future* (New York: Koehler Books, 2016).

AARP and Brandeis University Study on Women and Finance, April 2000.

Melinda Evans, quote relayed to us by Lori Sackler (see above).

37. WHEN DREAMS TURN TO DUST, VACUUM.

Arlan Hamilton, adapted from "How This Woman Went from Homelessness to Running a Multimillion-Dollar Venture Fund," *Inc Magazine,* August 2016, and "Salvador Rodrigues," *Inc. Magazine*, August 2016.

Leah Fessler, "The Improbable Rise of America's Hottest VC," accessed May 10, 2018 in the online publication *Quartz at Work.*

Charlotte Beers in conversation at Professional Business Women's Conference, San Francisco, California, March 2014.

Emily Canal, "Why Sara Blakely Thinks Being Underestimated Can Help Women in Business," *Inc. Magazine*, September 2017.

38. DON'T TAKE THE CRUMBS; YOU'RE HERE FOR THE WHOLE CAKE.

Caroline Myss, "Why Do You Settle for Less?" February 4, 2010, *http://www.oprah.com/spirit/why-do-you-settle-for-less-caroline-myss/all#ixzz5MerHK9D5*

Martin E. P. Seligman, "Building Resilience," *Harvard Business Review*, April 2011.

39. BE GRATEFUL THE DOG DIDN'T PEE ON THE CARPET.

Research and information provided to us by Dr. Robert Emmons, University of California Davis, April 2004.

CHAPTER 7: CARRYING WHAT CANNOT BE FIXED

Megan Devine, *It's OK That You're Not OK: Meeting Grief and Loss in a Culture That Doesn't Understand* (Boulder, CO: Sounds True Publishing, 2017), pp. 3–8.

47. PERSIST

Used with permission of the author. Dr. Judith Orloff, *Positive Energy* (New York: Harmony Books, A Division of Random House, December 2005).

50. REFUSE TO BE IMPRISONED BY YOUR PAST.

The International Resilience Project: Research and Application, Dr. Edith Grotberg. In Proceedings of the 53rd Annual Convention of ICP Cross-Cultural Encounters. Emily Miao (Ed). Taipei, Taiwan: General Innovation Service, 1996.

Martin E. P. Seligman, "Building Resilience," *Harvard Business Review*, April 2011.

52. SEEK OUT A DREAM CATCHER.

Dr. Ivan Scheier, "Rules for Dreamers," excerpted from the *Grapevine Volunteer Newsletter*, Sacramento, CA, April 1996.

54. FIND THREE WISE WOMEN.

Dr. Abraham Maslow and Deborah C. Stephens, *The Maslow Business Reader* (New York: John Wiley and Sons, 1999).

55. DISRUPT YOURSELF.

Whitney Johnson on *Invent Your Future* webinar with Deborah C. Stephens and in conversation at Indiana Conference for Women. Portions adapted from her book *Disrupt Yourself: Putting the Power of Disruptive Innovation to Work* (New York: Bibliomotion Inc., an impint of Taylor and Francis Group, 2015).

57. BE CURIOUS.

"This Simple Strategy to Help You Design the Life You Want," *Fast Company*, November 2016.

Bill Burnett and Dave Evans, *Designing Your Life: How to Build a Well-Lived, Joyful Life* (New York: Albert A. Knopf, 2018).

58. SHINE A LIGHT, DON'T CURSE THE DARK.

Jack Kornfield, *A Lamp in the Darkness: Illuminating the Path Through Difficult Times* (Boulder, CO: Sounds True Publishing, 2014), p. 8.

59. LEARN TO FORGIVE.

In conversation with Eva Kor, Indiana Conference for Women, 2018.

ABOUT THE AUTHORS

Deborah Collins Stephens is a best-selling author, leadership-development consultant, and executive coach. She resides in Bloomington, Indiana, with two adopted parakeets and a very old dachshund in a small house filled with hope.

Jackie Speier represents the 14th Congressional District of California in the US House of Representatives. Recently, *Newsweek* named her among the 150 most fearless women in the world. She has served in both the California State Senate and State Assembly. She lives with her family in the San Francisco Bay Area.

Jan Yanehiro is Director of the School of Communications and Media Technologies at the Academy of Art University in San Francisco. She has "right-sized" into a condo and is going "back to the future" by traveling to exotic lands—which reminds her of her first job out of college as an airline flight attendant.

Michealene Cristini Risley continues her work as a human rights activist. Her last film, *Tapestries of Hope*, explored the myth in Zimbabwe that if a man rapes a virgin he will cure his AIDS. The film won numerous awards and profiled activist Betty Makoni, who became a Top 10 CNN hero. Michealene is currently the CEO for Curiosity Ink Media, a kids' entertainment company. She lives with her family in Silicon Valley.

TO OUR READERS

santa clara
county
librarydistrict

Renewals: (800) 471-0991

www.sccl.org

> ## "A must-read for all women and the men who love them."
> —RITA MORENO

If you've ever felt overworked, overwhelmed, or just plain unlucky, this book is for you. Through this collection of stories, wisdom, and practical advice, readers will meet four ordinary women who have faced extraordinary life challenges. Together, they have a history of six marriages, ten children, four stepchildren, six dogs, two miscarriages, two cats, a failed adoption, widowhood, and foster parenthood. They have raised babies and teenagers together. They have built companies, lost companies, and sold companies. One of them was shot and left for dead on a tarmac in South America, and two lived through the death of their spouse. They have known celebrity and success along with loneliness and self-doubt.

This book started simply with four friends getting together at the kitchen table to talk about their lives. Week by week and story by story, they realized their support of each other could help other women struggling with life's myriad issues of work, family, and love, as well as the big questions of life and death. For over two decades, the power and strength of their collective friendship has enabled these women not only to survive but also to thrive. The remarkable results are in this collection of lessons and insights, which can help any woman turn any misfortunate event into a joy-filled opportunity.